Lecture Notes in Computer Science 1078

Edited by G. Goos, J. Hartmanis and J. van Leeuwen

Advisory Board: W. Brauer D. Gries J. Stoer

David Alex Lamb (Ed.)

Studies of
Software Design

ICSE'93 Workshop
Maltimore, Maryland, USA, May 17-18, 1993
Selected Papers

 Springer

Springer

Berlin
Heidelberg
New York
Barcelona
Budapest
Hong Kong
London
Milan
Paris
Santa Clara
Singapore
Tokyo

Series Editors

Gerhard Goos, Karlsruhe University, Germany

Juris Hartmanis, Cornell University, NY, USA

Jan van Leeuwen, Utrecht University, The Netherlands

Volume Editor

David Alex Lamb
Queen's University, Department of Computing and Information Science
Kingston, Ontario, Canada K7L 3N6

Cataloging-in-Publication data applied for

Die Deutsche Bibliothek - CIP-Einheitsaufnahme

Studies of software design : selected papers ; workshop / ICSE
'93, Baltimore, Maryland, USA, may 17 - 18, 1993. David Alex
Lamb (ed.). - Berlin ; Heidelberg ; New York ; Barcelona ;
Budapest ; Hong Kong ; London ; Milan ; Paris ; Santa Clara ;
Singapore ; Tokyo : Springer, 1996
  (Lecture notes in computer science ; Vol. 1078)
  ISBN 3-540-61285-8
NE: Lamb, David Alex [Hrsg.]; International Conference on Software
  Engineering <15, 1993, Baltimore, Md.>; GT

CR Subject Classification (1991): D.2-3, K.6

ISBN 3-540-61285-8 Springer-Verlag Berlin Heidelberg New York

© Springer-Verlag Berlin Heidelberg 1996
Printed in Germany

Typesetting: Camera-ready by author
SPIN 10512960   06/3142 – 5 4 3 2 1 0   Printed on acid-free paper

Contents

Part III: Design Methods

Introduction: Studies of Software Design

David Alex Lamb

Software Technology Laboratory
Department of Computing and Information Science
Queen's University
Kingston, Ontario, Canada K7L 3N6
dalamb@qucis.queensu.ca
http://qucis.queensu.ca/home/dalamb/

1 Motivation

This volume is the proceedings of the Workshop on Studies of Software Design held in Baltimore, Maryland May 17-18, 1993, co-located with the International Conference on Software Engineering. The idea for the workshop arose in discussions with colleagues at Queen's University regarding the potential value of small invitational workshops for building a community of researchers interested in a common set of problems. For some years I have been uncomfortable with computing people's use of the word "methodology," which has typically meant *the development or advocacy of particular methods*, when it *ought* to mean *the study of methods*. I hoped, in organizing a workshop on "studies" of software design, to discover or create a community of methodologists of the second kind.

This hope led to several key decisions about the workshop: to keep it small (at most 25 people), to allow significant time for discussion, and to prefer researchers with ready access to the Internet. The call for papers was distributed only electronically, primarily via the USENET newsgroup comp.software-eng.

The workshop provided an opportunity for those who study software designs and design methods to meet informally and exchange ideas. The emphasis was on methods for studying, analyzing, and comparing designs and design methods, rather than on specific design methods themselves. Furthermore, we focused primarily on the "software architecture" level of design, and on techniques suitable for dealing with large systems.

2 Overview

Before reviewing the individual papers, it is appropriate to summarize the perspective from which they were selected. In software, the word "design" has several distinct meanings. To "design" might mean:

1. to choose specific functionality for an incompletely specified requirement (more specifically, "requirements analysis and specification")
2. to decide exactly how the system will take inputs from, and present outputs to, its human users ("user interface design")

3. to decompose the system into a collection of interrelated parts (once called "preliminary design"; now, perhaps "software architecture")
4. to define the interface and precise behaviour of a small software component ("detailed design")
5. to create an algorithm and related data structures ("algorithm design")

For this workshop, we focused on meaning 3.

A system (of any kind, not necessarily software) is a collection of interrelated parts, separated from its environment by a boundary. A *software requirements specification* describes the "behaviour" of the system, which we can characterize as a description (one hopes, a precise one) of the interactions between the system and its environment. A *software design specification* (or "design") is a description of the parts, their connections and interrelationships, and their individual properties and behaviour. Ideally, it also includes a description of how the properties and behaviour of the overall system derives from that of the parts.

Designs are constrained by the need for human beings to understand them. They deal with higher levels of abstraction than program code, suppressing details so that what remains is within the cognitive abilities of the human designers and coders. A component must interact with relatively few other components, so that a human can understand those interactions.

If it is large, a requirements specification itself needs some form of division into parts. If this division is also suitable for the software design specification, the transition from requirements to design can be seen as evolutionary; otherwise, the new structures introduced during design require some type of transformation from, or tracing back to, the requirements.

A *software architecture* is a portion of a software design specification that focuses on the parts and their interactions with each other. The same software system may have several architectures, characterized by different kinds of components (modules at one level of abstraction, subsystems at another) and different kinds and granularities of interactions. Indeed, any regularity in the structure or behaviour of a system is potentially a part of its architecture. An *architectural style* bears the same relationship to an architecture as a schema does to a database: it defines a vocabulary of kinds of components and interactions, such as "objects and methods" or "pipes and filters." A *framework* is more specific than an architectural style but less so than a particular design; it describes a pattern, potentially consisting of many architectural components, which must be instantiated and refined to produce a particular system.

A *software design method* is a prescription for constructing software design specifications[1]. It typically defines the kinds of software component and relationship for designers to describe, the local and global characteristics a design must exhibit, and guidelines for designers in how to come up with their designs. It may also give a particular method of describing component behaviour.

For small systems, a designer can work with pen and paper, or marker and whiteboard. As the complexity of systems and their designs increase, it becomes

---

[1] Currently, "software design methodologies" are expected to prescribe how to analyze requirements and implement designs, in addition to how to produce designs.

necessary to use computer-based tools to create, examine, and modify designs. Some tools are tailored to do a single task. Others are formulated as *metasystems*: generic tools, parameterized by specifications of particular design methods. Any metasystem involves three levels of specification:

- the *meta level*, where the metasystem designer provides a generic data modeling method, tool system architecture, and generic tool set;
- the *environment level*, where the CASE tool designer defines specific data models for a particular design method;
- the *user level*, where a software designer uses the tools produced at the environment level to develop a particular design

3 The Papers

Topics in the call for papers included

- Methods for studying, analyzing, and comparing software architectures.
- Representations of software designs, especially those not tied to a particular design method.
- Properties of software designs, especially those that characterize or typify the method according to which the software was designed.
- Methods of reasoning about designs.

The papers accepted for the workshop fall into three broad groups: software architecture, tools and representations, and studies of particular design methods.

3.1 Architecture

In the last five years, software architecture has emerged as a focus of concerns in software design. Soni *et al.* argue that architectural concerns occur at several levels of abstraction representation of the software. Each level has its own components, connectors, and design criteria.

Shaw argues that architectural description methods have focussed too strongly on components, ignoring interconnections among components. She summarizes the difficulties with conventional approaches, where information about component interactions is scattered, and proposes a system composition model where connectors have the same status as components. Dean and Cordy, inspired by earlier work of Shaw's along these lines, propose a diagrammatic method of describing software architectures, where the pattern and type of interconnections can be used not only to describe particular architectures, but also to classify architectural styles.

Minsky argues that global regularities are essential for understanding large systems, but their global nature has typically caused their representation to be scattered throughout the system. He proposes a scheme for "law-governed architectures," which centralizes and makes explicit many kinds of regularity.

Garlan describes three complementary formalisms for specifying aspects of software architecture: a formal description for a particular system, a generic method for describing architectural styles, and the beginnings of a formal basis for reasoning about architectural issues.

Murphy and Notkin argue that object-oriented frameworks require better notations for describing structural and behavioural relationships among the objects and classes comprising them, and better methods for reducing dependencies.

3.2   Tools and Representations

Several papers discussed tools for manipulating design-level information. The first three papers describe metasystems (in the sense of Section 2).

Sorensen and Tremblay's *Metaview* metasystem is based on an entity-relationship-attribute-aggregate data modeling method; a graphical extension for generating diagrammatic representations; and a rule-based "environment transformation language" for translating among design representations and computing metrics. With it, they have built CASE tools for several software development methods.

Ryman's *4Thought* metasystem uses an entity-relationship-attribute data modeling method, with "workplaces" playing a similar role to Sorensen and Tremblay's aggregates; and a graphical query language, Graphlog, equivalent to a relational calculus with transitive closure, to describe derived relationships and to check for violations of a design method's integrity constraints

Kramer *et al.* use *ViewPoints* to integrate different software development methods for distributed system. A ViewPoint has five slots, representing representational knowledge (the notation or style of a method), development knowledge (work plan or development strategy), and specification knowledge (domain information, partial system description, and development history). Inter-ViewPoint rules can be used to check consistency between different ViewPoints.

Other tools presented at the conference, while not characterized as metasystems, nevertheless show interesting manipulations and representations of design-level information. Griswold and Bowdidge describe a tool for software restructuring, based on design-level transformations. From program text their tool constructs a graphical representation; operations on the graph, such as moving a box representing a function, are translated into textual restructuring operations, such as moving the code for the function from one module to another. Diaz-Herrera describes *Hierarchical Modular Diagrams* (HMD), a technique for graphically representing static design structures (import-export relationships) in a language-independent way. HMDs are meant to be both easy to construct during development, and easy to re-construct during reverse engineering.

3.3   Design Methods

Two papers studied particular design methods.

Hinchey combines traditional "structured" design methods, such as Jackson System Development, with formal methods, such as Receptive Process Theory.

The formal approach gives a framework for reasoning about the correctness and completeness of the structured methods.

Yuan and Patel evaluate popular six object-oriented methods (Booch, Coad/ Yourdon, Embley *et al.*, Rumbaugh *et al.*, Shlaer/Mellor, Wirfs-Brock *et al.*) according to their ability to support six perspectives on object-oriented analysis and design. They consider support for modeling data (object modeling), modeling dynamic behaviour (state modeling), modeling actions in the state model (process modeling), transforming the results of analysis into system architectures (design), and consistency among the various models (model integrity)

4 Discussion

The presentation chosen for this proceedings (architecture, tools, and methods) is not the only possible one; several other threads run through the workshop. Formal (that is to say, mathematical) methods have commonly been used to specify aspects of system behaviour. Several of the papers show alternative ways to use formal methods (particularly Ryman, Garlan, and Hinchey). Representation of design information shows up (as expected) in the design metasystems, but also in Dean and Cordy's diagrams, in Minsky's "laws," and Murphy and Notkin's concern for documenting frameworks.

The papers in this volume collectively suggest several future directions for studies of software design:

- Description (in machine-processable form) of idioms of design, whether they be laws, patterns, frameworks, or architectural styles. Such descriptions must capture components, connections, and behavioural relationships, and allow for specialization and parameterization.
- Metasystems for description and manipulation of architectural information. In the 1980's, abstract syntax trees proved a fruitful representation for programs; what are the equivalent methods for architectures?
- Connection of design-level descriptions of software systems "up" to requirements, "down" to implementations, and "across" to different architectural views of the same system.

5 Acknowledgments

Thanks especially to Sandra Crocker of Queen's University, who did all the administrative work for organizing the workshop, and to Marv Zelkowitz of the University of Maryland, who handled local arrangements. David Skillicorn of Queen's, Mary Shaw of Carnegie-Mellon, Naftaly Minsky of Rutgers, and Pamela Zave of ATT gave valuable advice while I was formulating the call for papers. The Information Technology Research Centre, an Ontario Centre of Excellence, provided much-appreciated partial funding for the workshop.

Many Faces of Software Architecture

Dilip Soni, Robert L. Nord, Liang Hsu, and Paul J. Drongowski

Siemens Corporate Research, Inc.
755 College Road East
Princeton, New Jersey 08540, USA
{dsoni, rnord, lhsu, pdrongowski}@scr.siemens.com

Abstract. One reason that hardware design is more systematic than software design is that hardware designers have reached agreements about the description levels for design artifacts. We hypothesize that quality and productivity in software development would be improved if software designers were to arrive at similar agreements. As a first step, we look at representations related to software architecture.

Since software architecture is an emerging field, the research community has developed little consensus on the definition of architecture except that architecture describes the structure of a system as composed from its subcomponents, and the interactions among them. To help us identify pragmatic issues related to architecture, we have surveyed a variety of systems to understand their structure and their use. In our study, we observed that many systems have more than one structure addressing different concerns related to system construction, functional and non-functional characteristics, and the development environment.

Based on these observations, we propose several different representation levels for software architecture. We briefly describe issues arising from multiple representations of software.

1   Introduction

One important distinction between hardware and software design is that hardware designers have reached agreements about the precise description of design artifacts which are separated into levels describing different concerns. As described in Fig. 1, such levels range from architecture to logic design to the physical level of layouts and masks [2]. This precision and separation allows the hardware designers to construct design editors for each level and tools to check consistency between levels [12]. Each level also serves a particular useful purpose in the design process.

Our hypothesis is that quality and productivity in software development would be improved if software designers were to arrive at similar agreements. In other words, we need to view a software system from a variety of perspectives, precisely describe these perspectives, separate these descriptions to manage complexity, establish correspondence, and facilitate the analysis and manipulation of these descriptions. We do not want to imply that informal descriptions of design are useless, however, we do believe that their usefulness is rather limited.

PMS Level	processors, memories, ...
Program Level: HLL	floating point processor, memory allocator, ...
Program Level: ISP	instruction decoding, processor state, ...
Logic Design: RTL	microstore, micro sequencer, registers, ...
Logic Design: Switching	gates, flip-flops, latches, ...
Circuit Design	transistors, resistors, capacitors, ...
Physical Level	layout, masks, fab process, ...

Fig. 1. Hardware representation levels

A naive way to arrive at such an agreement might be to define a collection of representation levels as described in Fig. 2, where a level corresponds to a software development life-cycle phase and its output. However, the current generation of methods and tools for software engineering provide no single point of reference for the diverse cares and concerns of the software developer. And, since there is little consensus on these life-cycle phases, such a characterization of representation levels is not going to help improve the state of the art. Any agreement on representation levels should be based on their contents rather than when they are produced.

We have taken an alternative approach, starting with software architecture, which focuses on the structure of a software system rather than on its function. When poorly understood, architectural aspects of design are major sources of errors. By focusing on these aspects, we will complement current approaches to design.

First we give a general definition of software architecture to set the context for our proposal. Then we propose several representation levels based on the synthesis of our observations. We compare this proposal to related work and discuss its implications. We conclude with a summary of our work in the area of software architecture.

Requirements	Natural Language, Structure Charts,...
Specification	Z, VDM, LOTOS, Larch,...
High-level Architecture	Pipe/Filter, Blackboard, Client/Server,...
High Level Design	Data Flow Diagrams, HIPO Charts,...
Detailed Architecture	MIL75, ADL, Unicon,...
Detailed Design	SDL, State Charts, FSMs, ...
Implementation	Source Code, LEX/YACC,...

Fig. 2. Software representation levels: A naive view

2   Software Architecture

The distinction between many of the conventional design artifacts and software architecture is their focus on function versus structure. Software architecture describes the structure of a software system in terms of its decomposition into components and the relationships among these components. Relationships among components describe how the components are interconnected and how they communicate and interact with each other.

First, it is important to distinguish between architectures and architectural styles. An architectural style describes an abstract set of architectural elements and guidelines on how to construct a system while an architecture describes the structure or form of a particular system constructed using a software architectural style for a particular software system. An architectural style may evolve over time with experience and new technology. An architecture of a system may also optionally evolve with the architecture styles.

We define *software architecture* as <structure, interactions> where

- The *structure* describes the decomposition of the system into its components.
- The *interactions* describe the interconnections and protocols among the components of a system.

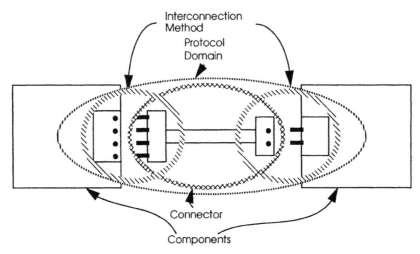

Fig. 3. Components and connectors

We define a *software architectural style*[1] as
<components, connectors, design criteria> where

- A *component* represents some complex functionality with optional state. Data Collector, Data Analyzer, Display Manager, and Report Generator are some examples of components. Another example of a component is an operation with operands. A component's implementation and interface may be affected by how it is connected to other components,[2] that is, whether it is to be invoked as a procedure call or as a remote procedure call or through message passing or through an interrupt or an event.

- A *connector* connects two or more components using a particular *interconnection method*, following a particular well-defined *protocol* (see Fig. 3). Pipes, Persistent Storage, and Asynchronous Message Bus are some examples of connectors. A connector includes a syntactic aspect which corresponds to an interconnection method and a semantic aspect which corresponds to a protocol.

  - An *interconnection method* describes how a connector is connected to other connectors and components.

  - A *protocol* is the set of agreements among connectors and components relating to the format and relative timing of information to be shared, exchanged, and processed, the ordering of actions and the recovery from errors.[3] Informally, a protocol describes how com-

---

1. The way we define our architectural style is similar to that defined by Perry and Wolf [15].
2. This is one major reason why developers need to modify the implementation of a component while reusing it in another system - even when its specification is unchanged.
3. This is an adaptation of the definition from [3]: "When we have two processes facing each other across some communication link, the protocol is the set of their agreements on the format and the relative timing of messages to be exchanged."

ponents and connectors coordinate and synchronize their interactions and communicate with each other.

An example of a protocol is the Inter-Client Communication Conventions for the X Window System [19]. This protocol describes conventions for communication between applications and window managers, for example, how to resize a window, exchange information, and what to do when the window manager refuses a service. Before this protocol was developed it was not possible to run arbitrary applications with arbitrary window managers.

- The *design criteria* consist of heuristics for the selection and use of components and connectors, their decomposition, and constraints on the topology of their interconnection.

3   Software Representation Levels

To help us identify and focus on pragmatic and concrete issues related to design and development of large systems, we conducted a survey of a variety of architectures used within Siemens [22]. These include several medical image processing systems, real-time Unix, communication systems, and instrumentation and control systems for power plants. In our study, we observed that many systems have more than one structure addressing different concerns related to system construction, functional and non-functional characteristics, and the development environment.

Based on our discussions with system architects and developers of these systems, we propose five levels of representation based on software architecture and source code (see Fig. 4). These five levels can be and are often quite different in many systems. They are different in their structural relationships, in their criteria for decomposition, and in the way they are used in the design process.

The base representation level of a software system is the source code. At present, this is the only representation level that is always up-to-date and current. What a system does is often defined by its source code. All of the architecture representation levels manifest themselves, in one way or other, in the source code representation level. In order to make any significant impact on software development problems, any new representation levels must be related or traceable to this level.

The principal components in source code are the procedures which are connected via procedure calls. The interconnection method of a procedure call is the name of the procedure and the parameters (including the ordering and naming). The protocol behind this primitive connector includes the conventions about whether the caller or callee saves the registers, how the parameters are passed, where the return address is located, and how the results are returned to the caller.

The second level represents how the source code has been organized into files, directories, linker libraries, and executables. For programming languages such as Ada, this level also includes packages and program libraries. We call this represen-

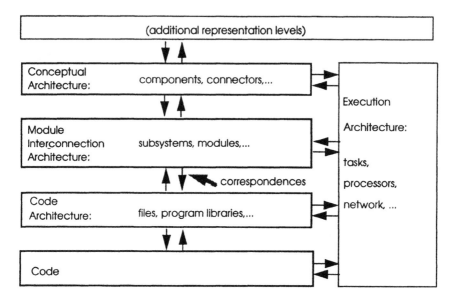

Fig. 4. Architecture-based software representation levels

tation level the *code architecture* of a system. It is sometimes called the *static product structure*. The code architecture is mainly influenced by programming languages used in the implementation, development tools, and the development environment. It is used for interface checking, systems building, configuration management, and packaging of the system for a variety of customers.

The third representation level describes the system in terms of its logical decomposition into subsystems, modules, and layers along with their interrelationships in terms of exported and imported interfaces. This can be viewed as an *ideal product structure* of a system. We call this level the *module interconnection architecture*. Module interconnection architectures are used to describe, control, and manage module interfaces in code. They are also used to facilitate independent construction and testing of various subsystems.

The fourth representation level describes the dynamic aspects of a system in terms of its active agents (e.g., processes and tasks) and resource allocation (e.g., assignment of functional components to tasks and assignment of tasks to processors). It can also be called a *dynamic product structure*. Communication and interfaces among components are determined by this assignment and the underlying network and inter-process communication mechanisms. We call this level the *execution architecture* of a system. The execution architecture is mainly influenced by the runtime environment, including the underlying hardware platform, operating system, and inter-process communication. It is used to enable partitioning of system functionality into such processes as servers and clients and for performance and schedulability analysis. The dynamic product structure is sometimes trivial, for example, when the system is a single process.

The fifth representation level describes the system in terms of components representing its major design elements, and connectors representing interrelationships between components. This is a very high level and domain-specific perspective of the system, using objects, relationships, and protocols of the application domain. We call this level the *conceptual architecture* of a system. Conceptual architectures are used to enable assignment and partitioning of system functionality, and to specify and analyze domain-specific system properties.

Work at the conceptual level has been done in the domain of industrial control systems [8]. All components are quite simple and perform a well defined mathematical or control function. The connectors, along with synchronization and communications are the most complex parts of the software. Fischer has demonstrated how it is possible to take advantage of the constraints and restrictions of the domain of safety-critical control to analyze the designs and generate code based on the system description. He also emphasizes the role of execution architecture in code generation. When design is complete, components are assigned to individual processors before code is generated. Compilation is based on the manual implementation of primitive components. Code for complex synchronization and communication protocols is localized.

Architectural styles exist for all of the representation levels of architecture. Table 1 gives examples for some of the components, connectors, and design criteria used in each of the levels.

4   Related Work

In some ways, these representations can be related back to the history of Software Engineering. At first, only the source code existed. Then interfaces were introduced for type checking by compilers or other tools. As software became larger it became useful to divide work into files and introduce information hiding techniques. "Make," configuration management, and systems building techniques were introduced along with a flexible product structure to describe and manipulate the file level organization of source code [7, 6, 13].

As systems became even larger and multiple programmers worked on a project, abstraction mechanisms, modules, and module interconnection languages were introduced. The importance of module interconnection architectures for programming-in-the-large was first recognized by DeRemer and Kron [5]. Several variants of module interconnection architectures have been defined with associated languages to describe them [23, 24, 16, 14].

When systems became distributed, programmers needed to consider the dynamic structure and communication, coordination, and synchronization. Functional components needed to be allocated within the dynamic structure [11]. Recently a number of languages based on allocating components in a distributed environment have been introduced. These include Durra [1], Polylith [17], and SALE [18].

Table 1. Examples of Architectural Elements

Software Representation Level	Components	Connectors	Design Criteria
Source Code	program units such as procedures, types, constants, and variables,	procedure calls	semantics of program language, functional decomposition methods, criteria such as information hiding and abstraction
Code Architecture (Static Product Structure)	files, directories, linker libraries, packages, program libraries	member_of, includes, contains, linked_with, compiled_into, with clause, use clause	semantics of file system, criteria related to project management and configuration management tools and the development environment
Module Interconnection Architecture (Ideal Product Structure)	systems, subsystems, modules, layers	component_of, import, export	when to use multiple interfaces, constraints imposed by layering strategy
Execution Architecture (Dynamic Product Structure)	executables, tasks, threads, processes, clients, servers, processors	interprocess communication such as IPC, RPC, networks	criteria for priority assignment, constraints imposed by runtime environment
Conceptual Architecture	domain-specific components	domain-specific interconnections, protocols	constraints on cycles, requirements on throughput

Now research is progressing to higher abstraction levels [20, 4, 9]. Software engineers would like to be able to compose software systems as if they were assembling components. In order to be practical, this level must be related back to the previous representation levels.

The challenge, as we see it, is to precisely describe these representations, separate their descriptions to manage complexity, establish correspondences between the descriptions, and facilitate analysis and manipulation of the descriptions. Our contribution has been in emphasizing the existence of a the variety of architectural structures and proposing levels of representations to describe them.

5   Past, Current, and Future Work

Multiple representations are quite common in software systems. Source code, object code, lex and yacc sources, and executables are examples of software representations. Other examples are documents describing requirements, design, test plans and test suites. The first set of representations are easier to deal with because only one of them is created manually and the rest are automatically generated. Inconsistencies among such representations can be addressed using well known configuration management techniques. The second set of representations are only informally related to each other and to the first set of representations. The most "precise" relationship among all of these representations is generally established using conventions and version and configuration management.

When several of the representations can be independently created, several issues arise:

- Precise and unambiguous notations or languages are needed to describe and model the representations. It is still an open research issue whether a single language would be sufficient for this purpose.

- To achieve advantages similar to those in hardware design, we need to relate these representations to source code. How do we establish correspondences among these representations?

- All of the representations are not entirely independent of each other. When one of them is modified independently of another, inconsistencies are likely to arise. There are two ways to deal with such inconsistencies:

    - Disallow inconsistencies: This can be supported by an integrated representation editor which prevents a user from making modifications which may be inconsistent with other representations. This is the approach followed by many of the CAD environments.

    - Check for inconsistencies: This can be supported by establishing correspondences among representations and checking them at the request of the user. The decision to allow them or not is then left up to the policies of the development organization. This is the approach followed by many software development environments.

- Can these representations be analyzed for non-functional properties such as performance and schedulability?

- Is it possible to generate parts of one representation based on parts of another?

We are addressing these issues in our research program. We plan to develop a design method based on these different descriptions that is practical and that will scale. We plan to demonstrate the usefulness of our methods and tools on small to medium scale systems initially. Our research will be evaluated by how well we are able to use our methods and tools in our case studies.

In a previous project [21, 10], we built a prototype for describing software systems in three representation levels: source code, code architecture, and module interconnection architecture. We precisely described a window manager (40 KLOC) in these three levels and established correspondences among them. The prototype, with the help of these correspondences, checks the consistency between the different levels, and assists in making corresponding changes to all three of the representation levels.

In our current work, we are adding the perspectives of conceptual and execution architectures. For this purpose, we have selected Cardiac Station, a computer-based medical system from Siemens Medical Systems. We are planning to demonstrate the usefulness of our design methods and tools in the design, analysis, implementation, and maintenance of this system. In the course of our work, we are investigating different strategies for system decomposition, interconnection, and analysis that are important within specific application domains and how these strategies are used in software development. We are also investigating how to manage the use of software architectures in the development process and how to detect violations of architectural constraints in the implementation.

In the long run, we plan to develop a product-specific workbench for an application such as patient monitoring, telephone switching, or industrial control. An architect's workbench would support "what if" experiments for the evaluation of design alternatives, selection of objects from a library of well-characterized components and connectors, and partial compilation of the design into its implementation. The workbench would also assist the adaptation of existing designs, code and test data for new features or infra-structural requirements.

References

[1] Barbacci, M.R., Weinstock, C.B., Wing, J.M.: Programming at the processor-memory-switch level. In *Proceedings of the 10th International Conference on Software Engineering*, IEEE Computer Society Press (April 1988) 19-28

[2] Bell, C.G., Newell, A: Computer Structures: Readings and Examples. McGraw-Hill (1971)

[3] Crocker, S.D. et al.: Function-oriented protocols for the ARPA computer network. In *Proceedings AFIPS*, Spring Joint Computer Conference (1972)

[4] Delisle, N., Garlan, D.: Applying formal specification to industrial problems: A specification of an oscilloscope. *IEEE Software* (September 1990)

[5] DeRemer, F., Kron, H.: Programming-in-the-large versus programming-in-the-small. *IEEE Transactions on Software Engineering*, **SE-2**, 2 (June 1976) 80-86

[6] Feiler, P.: Configuration management models in commercial environments. Technical Report CMU/SEI-91-TR-7, Carnegie Mellon University (1991)

[7] Feldman, S.I.: Make - a program for maintaining computer programs. *Software - Practice and Experience* **9** (November 1979) 255-265

[8] Fischer, H.D.: Special features of a computer-based German reactor protection system. In *Proceedings of Fault-Tolerant Computing Systems*, Springer-Verlag, Nürnberg (September 1991) 266-287

[9] Garlan, D., Shaw, M.: An introduction to software architecture. V. Ambriola and G. Tortora, editors, In *Advances in Software Engineering and Knowledge Engineering*, Volume I, World Scientific Publishing Company, New Jersey (1993)

[10] Greenberg, M., Soni, D.: Change Assistant: An editor for programming-in-the-large (in preparation)

[11] Hatley, D.J., Pirbhai, I.A.: Strategies for Real-Time System Specification. Dorset House Publishing, New York (1988)

[12] Katz, R.H.: Information Management for Engineering Design. Springer-Verlag (1985)

[13] Lange, R., Schwanke, R.W.: Software architecture analysis: A case study. In *Proceedings of the Third International Workshop on Software Configuration Management*, Trondheim, Norway, ACM Press (June 1991)

[14] Narayanaswamy, K., Scacchi, W.: Maintaining configurations of evolving software systems. *IEEE Transactions on Software Engineering* **SE-13**, 3 (March 1987)

[15] Perry, D.E., Wolf, A.L.: Foundations for the study of software architecture. *ACM SIGSOFT Software Engineering Notes* **17**, 4 (October 1992) 40-52

[16] Prieto-Diaz, R., Neighbors, J.M.: Module interconnection languages. *The Journal of Systems and Software* **6**, 4 (November 1986) 307-334

[17] Purtilo, J.M.: The polylith software bus. Technical Report UMIACS-TR-90-65, University of Maryland (May 1990)

[18] Royce, W.: TRW's Ada process model for incremental development of large software systems. In *Proceedings of the 12th International Conference on Software Engineering*, IEEE Computer Society Press (March 1990) 2-11

[19] Scheifler, R.W., Gettys, J.: X window system. Digital Press, Bedford, MA (1990)

[20] Shaw, M.: Larger scale systems require higher level abstractions. In *Proceedings of the Fifth International Workshop on Software Specification and Design*, IEEE Computer Society, Software Engineering Notes **14**, 3 (May 1989) 143-146

[21] Soni, D.: Intelligent support for software maintenance. In *Siemens Review*, (Spring 1991) 14-18

[22] Soni, D., Nord, R.L., Hsu, L.: An empirical approach to software architectures. In *Proceedings of the Seventh International Workshop on Software Specification and Design*, IEEE Computer Society (December 1993) 47-51

[23] Tichy, W.: Software development control based on module interconnection. In *Proceedings of the Third International Conference on Software Engineering*, IEEE Computer Society Press (May 1979) 29-41

[24] Wolf, A.: Language and tool support for precise interface control. Technical Report COINS-TR-85-23, University of Massachusetts (1985)

Procedure Calls Are the Assembly Language
of Software Interconnection:
Connectors Deserve First-Class Status

Mary Shaw[1]

Carnegie Mellon University

Pittsburgh PA 15213

Abstract

Software designers compose systems from components written in some programming language. They regularly describe systems using abstract patterns and
sophisticated relations among components. However, the configuration tools at
their disposal restrict them to composition mechanisms directly supported by the
programming language. To remedy this lack of expressiveness, we must elevate
the relations among components to first-class entities of the system, entitled to
their own specifications and abstractions.

Architectural descriptions treat software systems as compositions of components.
They focus on the components, leaving the description of interactions among these
components implicit, distributed, and difficult to identify. If the interfaces to the
components are explicit, they usually consist of import/export lists of procedures and
data. Interactions are expressed implicitly through `include` files or `import` and
`export` statements, together with the documentation that accompanies various libraries. This view of software architecture organizes information around the components and ignores the significance of interactions and connections among the modules.

This paper begins by discussing the limitations of the conventional approach to system configuration. It then argues that designers must attend as carefully to connections among components as to the components themselves. It closes by proposing a
model of system composition in which connectors are first-class entities along with
components. Section 1 summarizes current practice and Section 2 describes some of
the resulting difficulties. Section 3 gives a fresh view of system configuration and
Section 4 sketches a language to support that view.

---

[1]This research was supported by the Carnegie Mellon University School of Computer
Science and Software Engineering Institute (which is sponsored by the U.S. Department of
Defense) and by a grant from Siemens Corporate Research. The views and conclusions
contained in this document are those of the author and should not be interpreted as representing the official policies of any of the sponsors.

1. Current practice

When a designer writes a paper about a software system, the first section often includes a diagram and a few paragraphs of text labeled the "software architecture." The text refers informally to common software notions such as pipelines, client-server relations, interpreters, message-passing systems, and event handlers. The diagram usually consists of boxes and lines, but the semantics of the graphic elements varies substantially from one figure to another [5]. Figure 1 is typical of these figures. It depicts a sequence of three processing steps in which the second step also uses four abstract data types and communicates in various ways with a satellite, an interactive workstation, and a database. The components depicted in the diagram may have substructure, but ultimately the implementations of the components must be written in conventional programming languages.

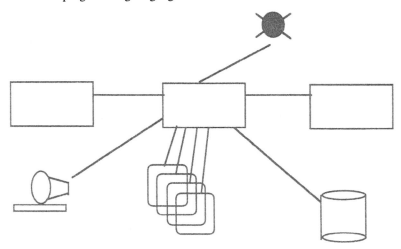

Figure 1: Typical box-and-line depiction of a software architecture

Sometimes components have explicit interface definitions. These define the external structure of the components. They usually consist of lists of procedures, exported data, and perhaps types, exceptions, etc. Ada's specification parts and C's .h files are examples of such interface definitions. Interfaces do not aggregate these details to reflect the more abstract relations they implement. The specifications of functionality, if any, are generally written in prose; formal specifications that provide details beyond type and signature are relatively rare.

In these conventional designs, all modules have equal status. That is, they are undifferentiated collections of procedures, data, and other constructs of the underlying programming language. Nothing analogous to a type system indicates that a module has special properties, discriminates among different kinds of modules, or identifies specific kinds of analysis available. In the associated implementations, import and export statements in each module establish the dependencies among modules. In

Ada these are uses clauses; in C they are includes. Specific associations, for example between a procedure definition and its call, rely on matching the names at the definition and use sites.

The models implicit in designers' architectural descriptions (both text and diagrams) do not match the actual realization of these models in code: Architectural models are rich, abstract, spontaneous, and almost wholly informal. However, the implementation languages, including module interconnection languages, are rigorous, precisely defined, and limited in expressiveness to the constructs of the underlying programming language.

As a result of these mismatches, the code fails to capture designers' intentions for the software explicitly and accurately and precise design documentation does not persist into maintenance. This impedes immediate checking and future guidance for development and maintenance activities. Even insofar as the code actually captures parts of the design, it does so in a highly distributed fashion, and it is hard for a reader to get a system-level overview. The need to address abstractions for system configuration is becoming widely recognized [3, 5, 6, 9, 10].

2. Problems with current practice

Current practice in architectural, or system-level, design focuses on components. For a system to work well, however, the relations among components, or *connectors*, require as much design and development attention as the components.

Connectors are less obviously objects of design than are components. After all, the connectors often do not have code—hence identity—of their own. They may be realized in distributed fashion by a variety of system mechanisms. Indeed, system mechanisms such as common scheduling and synchronization policies or the available communications protocols may constrain the designers' choices. Many of the problems with current techniques for architectural definition revolve around inadequacies of the mechanisms for defining component interconnection.

This section reviews some of the problems with the conventional approach of embedding the interactions among components within the components.

2.1. Inability to localize information about interactions

Most current module interconnection techniques, including programming languages such as Ada, depend on import and export commands lodged in the code modules of the system [4, 7]. A link editor then connects the components by matching the names of exported and imported constructs, possibly with guidance from the import and export statements about the scope of names. This has three major problems

- *Forced agreement in spelling:* The importer must use the same name as the exporter. In at least one case, a "reusable" library was not usable because its names conflicted with existing names of a system.

- *Dispersion of structural information:* An import/export strategy distributes structural information throughout the system. This hides the system structure and impedes reuse by creating embedded references to other components.

- *Forced asymmetry of interaction:* The import/export model assumes asymmetrical relations—there must be an owner and a user, or a master and a slave, or a source and a destination. Although many interactions are binary and asymmetrical, not all are: peer-to-peer communication is symmetrical, client-server relations can have multiple components in each role.

Current practice is also unable to localize the related abstractions. There is no natural home for the definitions that govern a class of interactions. Interactions are provided and defined by the operating system, the programming language, subroutine libraries, embedded languages, and ad hoc user-defined mechanisms. Giving legitimate, uniform status to definitions of interactions would improve system understanding and analysis.

2.2. Poor Abstractions

Boxes, lines, and adjacency don't have consistent meaning across system structure diagrams. They usually represent abstract interactions rather than the procedure calls and data declarations of the code. Practical systems have quite sophisticated rules about component interaction and shared representations. Existing definition mechanisms don't allow those design decisions to be captured in the code, so they can't be exploited for analysis or maintenance. The abstractions are hidden for several reasons:

- *Inability to associate related elements and name the cluster:* A module interface may export a large number of named elements. Apart from comments—which have no force—there is no good way to declare that a set of these elements behaves as a coordinated group. Further, there is no way to name the cluster for reference as a whole.

- *Inability to specify relations among related elements:* The ordering and state consistency requirements among a coherent set of calls are usually implicit. This is almost inevitable, for there is no logical place to state them.

- *Inability to specify aggregate properties of a collection of elements:* Even without explicit names, practical systems have quite sophisticated rules about protocols and shared representations. Individual procedure and data element specifications localize information and are not adequate to express these relations.

In Figure 1, shapes help the reader differentiate among different kinds of components, even though the programming language and module interconnection language may not support the distinctions. However, all the connections in that figure are represented in the same way—as simple lines. Figure 2 shows an improved drawing, with different line textures denoting different kinds of interactions.

Designers have abstract, sophisticated intentions for the relations among components. However, they have no reasonable way to capture these design intentions as a permanent part of the software. Even worse, the abstract relations are almost always realized as sequences of procedure calls embedded in modules whose ostensible function is something entirely different. Usual practice does not identify the abstract functions of the procedure calls, nor does it explain the rules about required order of operations.

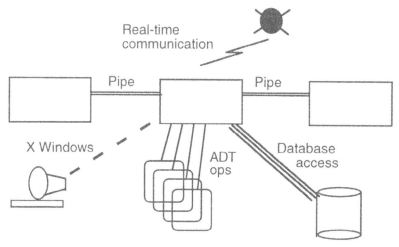

Figure 2: Revised architecture diagram with discrimination among connections

2.3. Lack of structure on interface definitions

As noted above, we lack a widely-used notation for structuring interface definitions so that they cluster coherent subsets of operations. In practice, though, a module is likely to have interfaces for one or more sets of primary users (to provide the overt system function) and additional special operations for such special uses as audit trails, monthly reports, executive control (setpoints or system tuning), system initialization, monitoring, and debugging. Monolithic interfaces can neither clarify nor enforce these distinctions.

Two levels of structure and abstraction are missing:

- *Abstractions for connections:* aggregation of primitive import/exports to show the intended abstract function of the connection.
- *Segmentation of interfaces:* decomposition of an interface into more-or-less conventional segments corresponding to different groups of users or different classes of functionality; each of these may involve several abstract connections.

2.4. Mixed concerns in programming language specification

Programming languages were designed to describe algorithmic operations on data. They are very good at defining data structures and algorithms that operate on those data structures. Extensions allow them to describe computational structures such as concurrency. They are not particularly good at describing reliability, absolute time, and a variety of extra-functional properties. Nor are they good at defining interactions among other modules that are more abstract than procedure calls and shared data.

Two problems result. First, all interactions not directly supported by the programming language must be encoded as sequences of procedure calls. Second, constructs for system composition have been grafted onto programming languages, with less than ideal results (e.g., `private` parts of Ada).

The concerns of architectural design are not with algorithms and data structures, but rather with system topology, assignment of capability to components, interactions among components, and performance characteristics. Therefore it is unrealistic to expect conventional programming languages to serve. Much of the current awkwardness seems to arise from attempts to add capabilities to conventional programming languages that stretch them beyond their design limits.

2.5. Poor support for components with incompatible packaging

When multiple components are reused—for example from different libraries—their interfaces do not always mesh well, even if their computational capabilities are substantially compatible. For example,

- If a component is cast as a filter, it can't be used as procedure because it does I/O to pipes instead of through procedure parameters.
- If a component is cast interactively, it often can't be called by another program.
- If semantics are suitable but packaging details such as name and parameter order differ, the user must write ad hoc conversions.

Something akin to typing is going on here: to use a component, you need to know not only what it computes but also how it delivers that computation. In many of these cases, the incompatibilities can be overcome by introducing mediators that accommodate discrepancies between the protocol expected by the component and the protocol requested by the designer.

2.6. Poor support for multi-language or multi-paradigm systems

The connection between components is substantially independent of the programming languages of the components. For example, this is usually the case when the components run as separate processes. Connectors that work naturally in these cases include unix pipes and many message systems.

In other cases, the connection between components depends directly on the programming language. This is often the case when components share assumptions about runtime systems such as representations of data types.

The conditions under which components in different languages can interact musts be detailed in such a way that a system development tool can tell which connections are allowable, which can be mediated, and which cannot be supported.

Furthermore, tools intended to support one architectural paradigm—object management tools, unix shell—offer little assistance in creating a system that mixes different architectural idioms.

2.7. Poor support for legacy systems

Most software development now involves modification of existing systems. Most of these systems evolved without configuration tools any more sophisticated than, say, make. Syntactic tools make it possible to extract the signatures—the names and types of imported and exported entities. However, they offer no help in recovering the higher-level intentions such as which set of procedures collectively implements a given abstract protocol. Over half of system maintenance effort goes into deciphering what the software already does, so the inability to record and retain the designer's higher-level intentions about component interactions is a major cost generator.

3. A fresh view of software system composition

Systems are composed from identifiable components of various distinct types. The components interact in identifiable, distinct ways. *Components* roughly correspond to compilation units of conventional programming languages. *Connectors* mediate interactions among components; that is, they establish the rules that govern component interaction and specify any auxiliary mechanism required. Connectors do not in general correspond individually to compilation units; they manifest themselves as table entries, instructions to a linker, dynamic data structures, system calls, initialization parameters, servers that support multiple independent connections, and the like.

It is helpful to think of the connector as defining a set of *roles* that specific named entities of the components must *play*.

Software systems thus comprise two kinds of distinct, identifiable entities: *components* and *connectors*.

- *Components* are the locus of computation and state. Each component has an *interface specification* that defines its properties. These properties include the signatures and functionality of its resources together with global relations, performance properties, etc. Each is of some type or subtype (e.g., filter, memory, server). The specific named entities visible in the interface of a component are its *players*.

- *Connectors* are the locus of relations among components. They mediate interactions but are not "things" to be hooked up (they are, rather, the hookers-up). Each connector has a *protocol specification* that defines its properties. These properties include rules about the types of interfaces it is able to mediate for, assurances about properties of the interaction, rules about the order in which things happen, and commitments about the interaction such as ordering, performance, etc. Each is of some type or subtype (e.g., remote procedure call, pipeline, broadcast, event). The specific named entities visible in the protocol of a connector are *roles* to be satisfied (e.g., client, server).

Components may be either primitive or composite. Primitive components are usually code in the conventional programming language of your choice. Composite components define configurations in a notation independent of conventional programming languages. This notation must be able to identify the constituent components and connectors, match the connection points of components with roles of connectors, and check that the resulting compositions satisfy the specifications of both the components' interfaces and the connectors' protocols.

Similarly, connectors may be either primitive or composite. They are of many different kinds: shared data representations, remote procedure calls, data flow, document exchange standards, standardized network protocols. The set is rich enough to require a taxonomy to show relations among similar kinds of connectors. Primitive connectors may be implemented in a number of ways: as built-in mechanisms of programming languages (e.g., procedure calls associated by a linker); as system functions of the operating system (e.g., certain kinds of message passing); as library code in conventional programming languages (e.g., X/Motif); as shared data (e.g., Fortran COMMON or Jovial COMPOOL); as entries in task or routing tables; as a combination of library procedures and a single independent process for the connector (e.g., certain kinds of communication services); as interchange formats for static data (e.g., RTF); as initialization parameters (e.g., process priority in a real-time operating system) and probably in a variety of other ways. Composites may also appear in these diverse forms; we need (but do not yet have) ways to define them, as well.

Connectors are properly treated separately from components because:

- *Connectors may be quite sophisticated*, requiring elaborate definitions and complex specifications that deserve their own homes. In many cases, no single component is the appropriate location for a protocol specification.

- *The definition of a connector should be localized.* Just as good methodology requires a single location for the definition of a component, good methodology requires a single location for the definition of an interaction. This supports both design (especially analysis during design) and maintenance. Further, connectors can be rich enough for their definitions to deserve their own homes.

- *Some information about the system does not have a proper home in any component.* For example, in a real-time system it may be appropriate for tasks to declare their needs and for a separate scheduler to satisfy them.

- *Connectors are potentially abstract.* They may be parameterizable. They may define classes of interactions that require additional scripting at the time of instantiation. Users may wish to define their own connectors, to make their own specializations, of existing connectors, or to compose their own connectors. A single connector may be instantiated multiple times in a single system; for example, a multicast capability could support many distinct sets of communicating processes.

- *Connectors may require distributed system support:* The mechanism required by a connector is not always localized to individual uses. For example, a message passing system may require exactly one server per processor for any number of communicating processes.

- *Components should be independent.* The interface specification of a component should provide a complete specification of the capabilities of that component but remain silent on how it is actually used.

- *Connectors should be independent.* A single (high-level) connector might mediate relations for a dynamically changing set of components. Wiederhold describes such a scheme [11].

- *Relations among components are not fixed.* A component may be capable of being used differently by different kinds of connectors. For example, a client might be indifferent to whether its server is dedicated, shared, or distributed. In addition, system connectivity can change dynamically.

System compositions quite frequently reuse patterns of composition; some of these patterns are commonly understood, at least intuitively: pipe/filter, client/server, layered system, blackboard. These common idioms can be defined as generic patterns that restrict the types of components and connectors to be used and describe how the pattern is implemented [5]. This may involve constraining the topologies of interconnection. Current module interconnection languages are wholly inadequate to this task for reasons elaborated in Section 2.

4. An architectural language with first-class connectors

Software system composition involves different tasks from writing modules: the system designer defines roles and relationships rather than algorithms and data structures. These concerns are sufficiently different to require separate languages. The architectural language must support system configuration, independence of entities (hence reusability), abstraction, and analysis of properties ranging from functionality to security and reliability [9]. The design of such a language is not straightforward. In addition to having a syntax, it must:

- Define semantics for connectors and their compositions.
- Generalize the import/export rules to address asymmetry, multiplicity, locality, abstraction, and naming.
- Establish type structures for system organizations, components, connectors, and the primitive units of association of these elements; this includes defining taxonomies for the types.
- Set out appropriate rules for architectural abstractions.

This section contains some initial notes on these language design problems.

4.1. Language structure

As suggested above, the language needs separate (but parallel) constructs for components and connectors. It must provide notations for composition and a set of primitives (including primitives defined in conventional programming languages). For simplicity, the constructs for components and connectors can be similar. Figure 3 suggests the essential character of the language. Each construct is typed. It has a specification part and an implementation part. The specification part defines specific units of association to be used in system composition.

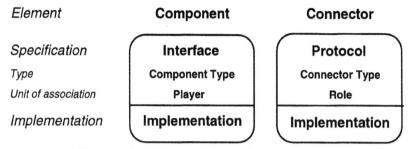

Figure 3: Gross structure of an architecture language

It is sometimes useful to say explicitly that an element is primitive; this means that it is not further defined at the architecture level but is implemented in a programming language or with system-level mechanisms.

For a nonprimitive element, the implementation part consists of a parts list, composition instructions, and related specifications. This establishes explicit associations and specification matches, thereby breaking free of name matching as the sole means of making connections.

The specifications should be "open" with respect to construction and analysis tools. Many different approaches are available for specifying and verifying system properties of interest; the languages should be able to accept those as uninterpreted expressions and interact appropriately with the specialized tools.

4.2. Connectors and their semantics

Most programming languages support some sort of intermodule connection. It usually supports only the primitive units of association of the language, such as procedure calls. Making the connectors first-class requires careful analysis of all the roles these constructs play in the definition of a system.

A connector mediates the interaction of two or more components. It is not in general implemented as a single unit of code to be composed. The previous section describes a number of the implementation possibilities. Whatever the implementation of a connector (especially an abstract one), detail about the implementation technique is encapsulated when the connector is used. Moreover, many or all connectors of the same type may share the same code or data. Allen is investigating formal specifications of the semantics of certain classes of connectors [1].

Like components, connectors require specifications. Specifications for connectors are called *protocols*. Since protocols can be of many different kinds, languages should allow for flexible specifications. One possibility is heavy use of property lists, with some standard attributes and some attributes specific to particular connector types. This allows for properties as diverse as:

- guarantees about delivery of packets in a communication system
- ordering restrictions on events using traces or path expressions
- incremental production/consumption rules about pipelines
- distinguishing between the roles of clients and servers
- parameter matching and binding rules for conventional procedure calls
- restrictions on parameter types that can be used for remote procedure calls

Primitive connectors include at least the ones directly supported by the programming language or operating system. These certainly include the procedure call and data accessors of each programming language; they also include language-specific process interactions such as the Ada `rendezvous`. Careful attention to the roles involved in primitive connectors show the need to support asymmetry: a procedure has a definer and multiple callers; data has an owner and multiple users. On the other hand, in certain classes of event systems all entities are equally entitled to generate and recognize events, so it is also necessary to define symmetric roles in a protocol. The usual import/export or provides/requires relation is too restrictive.

The simplest kind of abstract connector is binary (its protocol has two roles, for example definer and user). Some of these are direct analogs of the language-supported connectors, such as procedure call. At the architecture level the relation is often more abstract. For example, it may be desirable to separate from the definition of a procedure the decision about whether it is to be a local or remote procedure call.

N-ary connectors that involve multiple components are also important. These may be symmetrical, with all connected components playing the same role (e.g., multicast). They may (probably more commonly) be asymmetrical, with different roles for different components or sets of components (e.g., client-server systems).

Connectors are often implemented as sets of procedures. A set of procedures frequently has an associated set of rules or assumptions about how the procedures will be used. These rules are often highly implicit. They may restrict the order in which procedures are called or require relations among parameter values. These rules amount to protocols for the interaction. For example, the operations of an abstract data type are used as a bundle; they often have order restrictions such as "initialize must be called before anything else; push must be called at least as often as pop." Explicit restrictions may be expressed in various ways, as path expressions or traces for execution order restrictions. Although it's not conventional, it is useful to think of abstract data types as having a protocol that guides the use of the operations. This not only captures essentials such as execution order restrictions but also decouples the selection of the abstract type from the selection of an implementation. This is not unlike Larch's separation between abstract properties and actual implementations.

Figure 4 suggests the protocols required to construct the system of Figures 1 and 2. These protocols should exist as independent definitions in the computing environment. They may take parameters (including partial specifications) and may support several variants. When they are used, additional specifications may be needed to specialize the protocol or select a particular form.

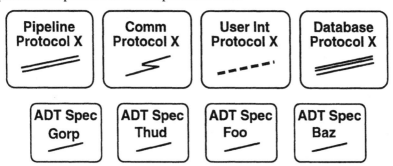

Figure 4: Constellation of protocol specifications required by example

Figure 5 shows some of the information that should be in the interface of the central component of Figures 1 and 2. This syntax is suggestive rather than definitive. Annotations on the left side show correspondences to the line styles of the diagram. Each of the nine lines of the interface describes an interaction with some other component. Note that in several cases the normal notion of exporting some resources and importing others does not apply well. For the pipes, additional specifications limit the type of information passing through the pipe. Similarly, a communication protocol may require additional specifications. The four abstract data types are all of the same general category of protocols; the bracketed names are the names by which the central component will call designated operations of the four types.

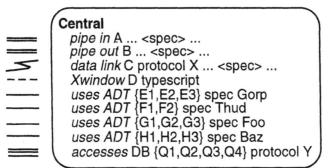

Figure 5: Interface specification of central component, referring to protocols

4.3. Architectural type structures

A problem akin to type checking arises at three points in an architectural language. Two appear in the preceding discussion: the types of components and of connectors.

As with any type system, these express the designer's intent about how to use the element properly. To be useful, they must also have some enforcement power.

Architectural types describe expected capabilities. They can limit the legitimate ways to use the construct. They can abbreviate restrictions on what can appear in the construct's specification. Examination of real systems shows that type hierarchies of this sort are useful. For example, there are many kinds of memories (components) and many kinds of event systems (connectors). Defining type structures for these elements requires creation of taxonomies that catalog and structure the type variations.

The third place where something like type checking shows up is at the actual point of associating *players* of components with *roles* of connectors. Each of the named entities in the interfaces (of components) and protocols (of connectors) must have enough type and other specification to check on whether the connector definition allows the components to be associated as requested.

Because of the need to reuse components and connectors in settings that aren't all quite alike, it is important to deal reasonably with associations that don't quite match. A very common example is the use of a unix pipe to send data to a file. The definition of a unix filter will probably say it's intended to interact with other filters through pipes. However, it is often (but not always) well-defined to substitute a file (passive component) for a filter (active component). The language must provide a way to define and control possible fix-ups, for example by supporting rules of the flavor "this pipe will accept a file in the role of filter under the following circumstances ...". Some of the interesting alternatives include:

- Associate anyhow: it will work without extra effort (some subtype relations).
- Rearrange or reformat information (data re-formatters [2], parameter re-mappers [8]).
- Wrap the component in a converter (a procedure wrapper for a filter would feed the input parameters to the input pipe of the filter and collect the result from the output pipe for delivery as a single value).
- Convert data to and from a shared form (interchange format).
- Convert data of one component to the form expected by another (pairwise compatibility; common message format, but data may need to be interpreted).
- Insert conversion module (buffer).
- Just say no.

The history of type coercion in conventional programming languages (especially PL/I) provides convincing evidence that this capability must remain firmly under control of the software designer at all times.

A special case of compatibility checking and enforcement arises when components are written in different programming languages. The difficulty of accomplishing this depends on the extent of the shared assumptions between the components.

- Sometimes there is no problem: One common easy case when two languages share runtime systems with common runtime representations, procedures, and protocols (Fortran/Snobol). A second common case is explicit, loosely-coupled interactions (unix pipes with ASCII streams).

- Sometimes the problem can be resolved with mediation as described above.

- Sometimes an external representation standard (RTF, PICT, SYLK) or an inter-language procedure call can serve as a cross-language connector.

- Sometimes it's simply too hard (languages with essentially different assumptions: rule-based; static imperative; dynamic).

4.4. Abstractions for higher-level connectors

The discussion so far has mentioned many different higher-level connectors. These include client/server relations, messages, event handlers, multicast communication, radio communication links, unix pipes, shared data, interaction through X/Motif or SQL scripts, hierarchical layers, and blackboards. The example of Figures 1 and 2 might be instantiated with SQL, X/Motif, various data abstractions with usage restrictions, unix pipes, and radio data links. The software development environment should provide the most common of these, either as part of the programming language, as basic operating system capability, or as part of the infrastructure (SQL, X/Motif). Protocols for this baseline collection should be primitive to the architectural language. It is still unclear exactly how to define the association of procedure calls with abstract protocols precisely, and the semantics of abstract connectors are also an open question at this time. However, it is clear that connectors have interesting internal structure, much as unix pipes contain buffers.

As discussed in section 2.3, component interfaces often have several distinct segments in order to establish different kinds of relations. Often these will have corresponding protocols.

An architectural language must support not only individual abstract connectors, but also high-level compositions that involve a number of connectors in specific relations to one another. For example, the language must be capable of capturing the high-level architectural idioms such as blackboards, interpreters, and various domain-specific architectures as abstractions. I conjecture that non-primitive connectors are the appropriate way to do this, but it isn't yet demonstrated.

5. The promise of explicit architectural notations

What makes the construction of composable systems different from conventional programming? First, composing a system from subsystems is unlike programming the algorithms and data structures that lie within the primitive subsystems. The semantics of the components, the locality of reasoning, the character of interaction with other components, the properties of interest, and the nature of the reasoning are all different. Second, we are liberating ourselves from thinking of the task as merely "programming". We are not merely building a program that receives inputs, executes, and terminates—we are building a system that has an enduring existence in some larger environment. Third, our units of manipulation are not simply conventional modules (which might export data, procedures, and perhaps tasks), but rather components and connectors.

Identifying connectors as first-class entities in a system can help to break us out of the programming-language mindblock for system composition languages. Legitimizing higher-level interactions among components allows us to understand the procedure call as one—perhaps the primary—primitive connector of pairs of modules. More significantly, it allows us to recognize higher-level connectors as critical to system design. We must learn to support higher-level connectors—composite components and connectors whose properties, expressed in their interface and protocol specifications, are as understandable as their constituents.

The view proposed in Sections 3 and 4 addresses the problems identified in Section 2.

- It specifically provides for localizing information about interactions: Nonprimitive components can invoke rich relations, and they concentrate structural information.

- It introduces abstractions for interactions and provides a starting point for user-defined abstractions and aggregations.

- It partially addresses the interface structure problem by using the *roles* of connectors to identify related operations as *players*.

- It separates architectural concerns from programming concerns by providing different language constructs with different semantics.

- It makes provisions for a type-checking system that can adapt to mild mismatches, thereby enhancing opportunities for reuse.

- It clarifies the conditions under which programming languages can be mixed.

- It offers prospects for improved support of legacy systems by making the architectural design of the system explicit.

The principled use of compositional structures should have a dramatic effect on software production. It should permit the choice of design paradigms to match desired system characteristics. It should allow the development of application-specific frameworks and reference architectures. It should provide the basis for exploiting compositional properties of systems for formal analysis, code generation, and software reuse. It should support a high level of visible abstraction for systems designers so that large systems can be more easily designed, understood, maintained and enhanced. It should enable us to better accommodate old code by providing ways to recover partial architectural information from existing systems.

Acknowledgments

These ideas have been evolving over a period of several years. They have been substantially sharpened and worked out in discussion with David Garlan over the past two years. Daniel Klein implemented the first prototype of the base language, Greg Zelesnik is extending the prototype, and Rob DeLine's critique stimulated clarification of the terminology. The CMU Software Architecture Reading Group has provided valuable feedback both on drafts of the paper and on the underlying ideas.

References

[1] Robert Allen and David Garlan. *Formalizing Architectural Connection. Proc. Sixteenth International Conference on Software Engineering*, 1994.

(2) Brian Beach. Connecting Software Components with Declarative Glue. *Proc. Fourteenth International Conference on Software Engineering*, 1992.

[3] Barry W. Boehm and William L. Scherlis. Megaprogramming. Proc. DARPA Software Technology Conference 1992, pp. 63-82.

(4) Frank DeRemer and Hans H. Kron. Programming-in-the-large versus Programming-in-the-small. *IEEE Transactions on Software Engineering*, SE-2(2):80-86, June 1976.

(5) David Garlan and Mary Shaw. *An Introduction to Software Architecture*. In V. Ambriola and G. Tortora (eds), Advances in Software Engineering and Knowledge Engineering, Volume I, World Scientific Publishing Company, 1993.

[6] Dewayne E. Perry and Alexander L. Wolf. Foundations for the Study of Software Architecture. *ACM SIGSOFT Software Engineering Notes*, vol 17, no 4, October 1992, pp. 40-52.

[7] R. Prieto-Diaz and J. M. Neighbors. Module Interconnection Languages. *Journal of Systems and Software* vol 6, no 4, November 1986, pp. 307-334.

(8) James Purtilo and Joanne Atlee. Module Reuse by Interface Adaptation. *Software: Practice and Experience*, 21(6): 539-556, June 1991.

(9) Mary Shaw and David Garlan. *Characteristics of Higher-Level Languages for Software Architecture*. Unpublished manuscript, 1993.

[10] Gio Wiederhold, Peter Wegner, and Stefano Ceri. *Toward Megaprogramming*. Stanford University Technical Report STAN-CS-90-1341, 1990.

(11) Gio Wiederhold. Mediators in the Architecture of Future Information Systems. *IEEE Computer*, 25(3):38-49, March 1992.

Software Structure Characterization Using Connectivity

Thomas R. Dean and James R. Cordy

Dept. of Computing and Information Science, Queen's University

Abstract. This paper presents a notation and taxonomy for characterizing software system structures based on their connectivity. The notation, based on typed multigraphs, provides both a diagrammatic syntax for describing system structures and a mechanism for specifying patterns of systems. We define a taxonomy of structure classes using sets of patterns. A system is a member of a structure class if its description in the notation matches a pattern for that structure class.

1. Introduction

This paper discusses the use of types of components to characterize software system structure. We provide a notation rich in structural types and a pattern mechanism based on the notation that is appropriate for describing structure and for building a taxonomy of system structures.

Our notation is a diagrammatic notation for system structure based on the types of components and the types of the connections between the components. One feature of the notation is that connections between the components are first–class entities. That is, the connections have an identity, and may be manipulated in ways similar to the other components. The notation is formalized using set theory, providing a means of defining operations on systems expressed in the notation. One of the operations we define is pattern matching, which we use for recognizing system structure.

Pattern matching provides a means of building a taxonomy of clearly defined, useful system structures. We show the effectiveness of our approach by building a preliminary version of a taxonomy. The structure classes identified by the taxonomy are derived from a sample of systems and system architectures from the computer literature.

A taxonomy constructed using our approach provides:

- A means of comparing system structure classes. Since the structure classes are derived from real systems, information is available about the strengths and weaknesses of each structure class.
- A framework for reasoning about system structure. The taxonomy requires a notation rich in structural constructs. This notation may be used to reason about system structure and provides the infrastructure to express other system properties such as behaviour.
- A method of classifying the structure of existing systems. Each element in the list of system structures is a canonical form of the structure class it represents.

- A syllabus of useful structures that may be used when designing new systems. Instead of emphasizing a single structure class, the designer can use different structures in separate parts of a system, choosing the structure that is most appropriate for the problem to be solved [Shaw89].

It should be emphasized that we are not characterizing the information exchanged between the structural elements. Instead, we are characterizing the types of elements and the types of the connections between those elements.

Mary Shaw [Shaw89] argues that larger systems require a higher level of abstraction. Larger and more complex systems are not easily handled using current techniques. She claims that identification of system structures and types is not sufficient; they must be codified consistently. Shaw notes that often, structure diagrams are used informally.

We use the types of the components to provide a framework to formalize such structure diagrams. In providing this framework, we distinguish between the structure of the system and the behaviour of the system. The structure of the system describes the way in which the system is organized. The behaviour of the system describes what tasks the system accomplishes. Both issues are important in software design.

An example of this split is the description of high–level languages such as C, Pascal and Ada. Each language is described in two parts. The first part is a context–free grammar that describes the structure of the language. The second part is a description of the behaviour of each of the structural components of the language. There are several advantages to this division between the structure and behaviour of high–level languages:

- We can identify classes of structural constructs (e.g., looping constructs).
- We can easily add new structural constructs to the language (e.g., modules).
- The structural definition provides a framework to discuss the behaviour of the types of elements and groups of elements (e.g., functions within modules).

The structure provided by these languages is important in the design, implementation and maintenance of systems written in the languages. The structural constructs of the language divide an existing system into identifiable parts, and simplify its understanding. As new design methods are developed, structural components are added to languages to help support translating the design to the implementation. Two examples are the module constructs of Turing and Ada, and the object oriented constructs of Smalltalk and C++.

This example makes two points. The first is that separation of structural representation is an important consideration in the design of any notation or abstraction technique. The other is that structural representation is an important tool in designing, implementing, understanding and maintaining systems.

Our research concentrates on the structure of large software systems given by their connectivity. That is, how groups of elements in large systems are organized and connected to each other. The purpose of our research is to build a taxonomy of clearly defined, useful system structures. The structure classes identified by the taxonomy are derived from a sample of systems from the computer literature.

Section 2 presents our notation for describing system structures. The pattern matching mechanism is described in Sec. 3. The taxonomy, explained in Sec. 4, consists of sets of patterns that identify particular structural classes. A system is classified by expressing its connection structure in the notation and then deciding which taxonomy patterns match the description.

2. Notation

Our notation is based on typed directed multigraphs. A typed directed multigraph provides typed nodes and typed edges and permits more than one edge of a given type between nodes. We extend the multigraph to allow edge types with arbitrary arity. Edges of these types may connect any number of nodes.

We have intentionally started with a limited number of types of elements. These have been chosen to show the flavour and flexibility of our approach. Other realizations of the approach may have more types of elements, either as separate types, or as subtypes of the existing elements.

While the focus of the notation is on the system structure, some (minimal) interpretation of the elements is necessary to motivate the choice of the types of nodes and edges. This interpretation is intentionally kept as broad as possible, so that it does not interfere with the structural analysis. The notation provides one type of active element, the task, and three types of inactive elements, all of which represent memory components. Tasks are characterized by their connections. Memory elements represent data repositories. There are six types of connection elements.

The tasks and memory elements are represented by the nodes of the graphs. The edges represent the connection components. Unidirectional and bidirectional edges are supported. The direction of the edge represents the intended direction of flow of information in the connection.

We use a diagrammatic representation of the notation, chosen so that system descriptions can be shown on a printed page. The next section describes the representation, and the following section its mathematical formalization. The representation is used to define concepts in the notation and present various characteristics of the notation.

2.1 Diagrammatic Representation

Figure 1 shows the visual representation of our element types. Lines are used to represent the edges of the graph. The type of edge is given by the visual characteristics of the line.

The nodes of the graph consist of circles and rectangles. Circles represent tasks and rectangles represent memory units. Different types of memory units have different types of rectangles. The three types of memory units are tables, random access repositories and files.

Table nodes are used to model static system data. They represent long term data that undergoes few, if any, changes. The random access repository (RAR) memory type models memory that changes rapidly and is accessed in many different ways (e.g., shared memory, databases). The file memory type is used to represent malleable persistent state. It models memory accessed sequentially.

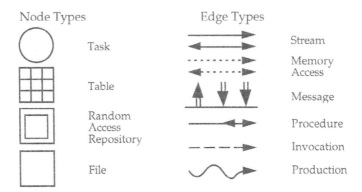

Fig. 1. Visual representations of notation elements

The connection primitives may be divided into two groups. The first group consists of stream, memory access, message and procedure. These primitives are used to communicate information. The other group contains invocation and production. They are used to model dynamic changes to the system structure. We describe each of the connection elements:

- Stream   Streams are binary connections between tasks. They indicate unidirectional or bidirectional direct communication between the tasks.

- Memory   The memory access connector is a binary operator between a task and a memory. As with the stream operator, it can be unidirectional or bidirectional.

- Message   The message communication primitive is a connector of arbitrary arity between tasks. A task may have two types of interaction with the message connector, send and receive. It may also have more than one of each type of connection with the same message connector.

- Procedure The procedure call primitive is a binary operator between two tasks and is used to model layered systems [Shaw89].

- Invocation The invocation primitive activates an existing task. Some startup information may be exchanged. An example would be the *fork* system call in the Unix operating system.

- Production The production connection primitive is used to represent the generation of one task by another. An example would be the link phase of a compilation.

As an example, Fig. 2 shows a representation of the canonical compiler structure used in undergraduate compiler courses. It is not a complete representation of a real compiler since the error stream is not represented, nor are multiple input files.

Elements of a system can be grouped together and abstracted into a single element that has the same external characteristics as the group. Our notation provides two aggregation mechanisms for nodes, heterogeneous and homogeneous aggregation. The symbol for heterogeneous aggregation is the hexagon.

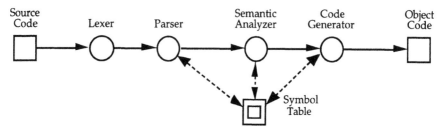

Fig. 2. Canonical compiler structure

Homogeneous aggregation is a special case of heterogeneous aggregation. When the only nodes inside the group that have connections outside the group are of the same type, homogeneous aggregation is used instead of heterogeneous aggregation. The group is replaced with a symbol of the same type.

Figure 3 shows two examples of aggregation. The first groups several memory nodes and a task using heterogeneous aggregation. The other uses homogeneous aggregation to abstract two tasks and a file.

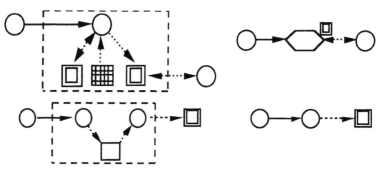

Fig. 3. Aggregation examples for nodes

Another type of grouping, metamorphic aggregation, is used to close a group of nodes into a connection. Figure 4 shows two examples of this form of aggregation. The first is a connection that translates a stream into a file. The other shows that metamorphic aggregation is not limited to binary connectors.

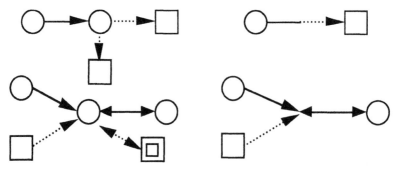

Fig. 4. Metamorphic aggregation for connectors

As with aggregation for nodes, there is a special case for metamorphic aggrega-tion. When there are two connectors involving nodes outside the system, and both connectors are the same type and direction, the new aggregated connector is identical. Figure 5 shows an example.

Fig. 5. Homogeneous aggregation for connectors

It is advantageous to reason about parts of systems separately. A partial, or in-complete, system is one in which not all edges are complete or it is indicated that an edge is required to incorporate the system into any other system. Only two types of incomplete systems are allowed: connection systems and subsystems. We define a connection system as a system that only contains incomplete edges. A subsystem is one that only contains indicated edges. These two types of partial systems correspond to the two groups of aggregation constructs provided by the notation. A connection system may be aggregated into a connection using metamorphic or homogeneous ag-gregation for connections. A subsystem may be aggregated using heterogeneous or homogeneous aggregation for nodes.

Indicated connections of subsystems may be thought of as variable connections. That is, they are place holders that may be bound to a connector to incorporate the subsystem into another system. Incomplete connection elements of connection sys-tems may be thought of as connecting one or more variable nodes. They may be used to connect two or more subsystems together by binding the indicated connections of the subsystems to the incomplete connections of the connection system, and the vari-able nodes of the connection system to nodes of the subsystems.

2.2 Mathematical Formalization

Our semantic model is based on set theory. Elements of the graph are represented using sets and relations. The primitives of the notation are represented using the fol-lowing sets:

N	The set of nodes in the system
C	The set of connectors in the system
MS	The set of message sites in the system
V	The set of variables in the system.

The nodes are the tasks and memory elements of the system. The set of message sites is used to handle multiple connections of the same message connector to the same task. The set of variables are the elements of N or C that are variables. Variable elements are used to handle incomplete systems. We define the tuple $EL = <N, C, MS, V>$ as the elements of the system.

Subsets of the sets in *EL* are used to establish types for each element. We define the tuple *Types* as the tuple containing all these subsets. There are four binary relations used to model the connection of the elements. These are:

src : N × C	Nodes are the source of binary connectors.
dst : N × C	Nodes are the destination of binary connectors.
has : N × MS	Nodes have message sites.
msg : MS × C	Message sites are associated with message connectors.

We define the tuple *Connections* = *<src, dst, has, msg>* as the connections of the system. A system is then defined as the tuple *System=<EL,Types,Connections>*.

We define restrictions on the sets and relations. A system is a valid system if and only if these restrictions hold for the model of the system. Figure 6 shows an example of a system and its translation. It is a subsystem, which means that it has indicated connectors. The indicated connectors are represented by variables. Only one of the source or destination relations are defined for each of these variables. In the example, the variable connectors *S1* and *BBA2* have destinations, but not sources.

We define several operations on graphs by defining them on the semantic model. One of these operations is *interface*. The *interface* operation takes a system and returns its interface. For a complete system, the interface of a system is a single task. For incomplete systems, the interface of a system is the aggregate of the entire system.

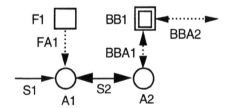

$N = \{ A1, A2, F1, BB1 \}$ $MS = \{ \}$
$C = \{ FA1, BBA1, BBA2, S1, S2 \}$ $V = \{ S1, BBA2 \}$
Task = { A1, A2 }   File = { F1 }   RAR = { BB1 }
Stream = { S1, S2 }   FileAcc = { FA1 }   RARAcc = { BBA1, BBA2 }
Read = { FA1 }   Write = { S1 }   BiDir = { S1, BBA1, BBA2 }
src = { <A1, FA1>, <A2, BBA1>, <A1, S2> }
dst = { <F1, FA1>, <BB1, BBA1>, <A1, S1>, <BB1, BBA2>, <A2, S2> }

Fig. 6. Example translation

3. Pattern Matching

Our taxonomy of system structures is specified using sets of graph patterns. A system described in the notation is an element of a taxonomy class if it can be matched by one or more of the patterns in the class set.

We start by defining two relations on systems: *equivalence* and *specialization*. We define pattern matching for simple patterns in terms of these relations. This definition is then extended to handle regular expressions and a form of context–free graph grammars. We then define a partial order on the patterns that match a given system description.

Two systems are *equivalent* if and only if they have the same interface. That is, two systems are equivalent if we can construct a bijection between the model representation of their interfaces such that:

- the types of all the related elements are the same and,
- any instances of the system relations (src, dst, has, msg) between elements of one interface hold between the related elements of the other interface.

We use the form A ≡ B if the system A is equivalent to the system B.

We define one interface as a *specialization* of another if we can construct an injection with the same properties as the equivalence bijection. That is, the interface is a subset of the other interface. We use the form $A \subseteq B$ if A is a specialization of B. We define *generalization* as the inverse of specialization. That is, system B is a generalization of system A iff system A is a specialization of system B. A system is a *minor system* of another if it is part of the other system. A *singular minor system* is a minor system that contains one element.

3.1 Direct Pattern Matching

We can now define the concept of a pattern match using the definitions of equivalence and singular minor systems. A system A is a *pattern* for another system B if A ≡ B and there exists an injection ϕ from the set of singular minor systems of P to the set of minor systems of Q such that:

- For all ϕ related minor systems A of P and B of Q, A ≡ B.
- The range of ϕ partitions Q.
- The ϕ related minor systems of Q are connected in the same way as the singular minor systems of P.

Figure 7 shows two systems, one of which is a pattern of the other. The pattern system is the system on the left and the matched system is the system on the right. The only non-singular minor subsystem in the match of the target system is formed by the two RARs and the task that connects them, and are shown in grey to identify them.

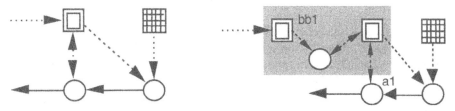

Fig. 7. Example pattern match

In practice, most systems will not be matched in their entirety by the taxonomy patterns. For example, the canonical compiler contains components that can be characterized as a pipe and filter system. It also has overlapping components that can be characterized as a shared memory system. Any useful method of characterizing system structures should be able to handle structures embedded within systems. We define a *subpattern match* as a matching of a pattern system to a system embedded within another system. Thus we can view the compiler as either an instance of a pipe and filter system or of a shared memory system. The definition is identical to pattern match except that specialization is used instead of equivalence, and the range of the injection does not have to partition the target system.

Although pattern and subpattern matching are useful, more expressive patterns are required. If, in the example in Fig. 7, a bidirectional memory access connection was added between the RAR *bb1* and the task *a1*, the pattern would no longer match. We add more flexibility to pattern matching in two steps. First, we define some simple repetition and alternation operators in Sec. 3.2. We then describe a restrictive form of graph grammars [FahBlo92] that may be used in expressing patterns in Sec. 3.3.

3.2 Regular Expressions

This section describes several pattern constructs that are equivalent to regular expressions. We start by defining an alternation construct, and add repetition and grouping constructs.

All of the connections in a pattern must be satisfied. All of the elements must be present in the target system for that pattern to match. The alternation operator allows us to choose between two or more alternative components of a pattern. Figure 8 shows the form of the alternation operator and two examples of its use. Only a binary version of the operator is shown, but it can be extended by adding as many lines a necessary to provide the appropriate number of choices.

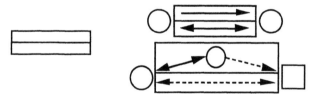

Fig. 8. Alternation and example uses.

The next step is to provide some optional and repetitive elements to the patterns. These are the '?', '*' and '+' operators. The definition of these operators is similar to that in conventional regular expressions. The '?' operator indicates that the element it is applied is optional. The '*' operator is used to specify zero or more instances of the element, and the '+' operator specifies one or more instances of the element. If the operator is applied to a connector, any instances of the connector connect the same elements and the connector. If they are applied to a node, an instance of each of the connections from that node to the rest of the system must be given for each instance of the node. Figure 9 shows two examples.

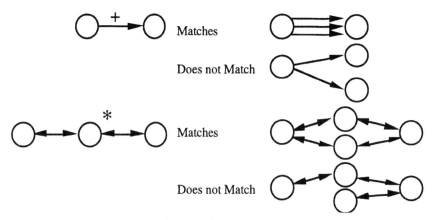

Fig. 9. Examples of replication.

The regular expression operator binds to the closest element. When the operator is near the point where a connection joins to a node, the operator applies to the node. Applying an operator to a node has a higher precedence than applying it to a connector. That is, when an optional or repetition operator is applied to a node and some of its connections, the result matches a system with an optional or repeated node, each of which has the optional or repeated connections.

In all of the cases presented so far, an element of the system matches if there is a minor system with the same interface. The '!' operator restricts the match to be a singular minor system. This operator may be applied to connectors and to any grammatical construct. It may also be combined with the '*', '?' and '+' operators.

The '*', '+', '?' and '!' operators bind to the closest single element. We provide two grouping operators that can change the way in which these operators specify the patterns. The behaviour of the group operators can only be distinguished when the '*' or '+' operators are applied. The first grouping operator is represented by a dashed polygon around the elements to be grouped. When the group is repeated, the pattern within the group may match any system it would match alone.

The second grouping operator is represented by a solid polygon around the elements. When this group is replicated, all of the repeated patterns must expand to the same primitive pattern. This group does not require those patterns to match the same system (i.e., some aggregation may occur), but the final pattern system must be identical in all repeated elements.

Figures 10 and 11 show two examples of patterns using some of these operators. Figure 10 shows the pattern of a central repository system and an example system that matches the pattern.

Figure 11 shows the pattern for a distributed repository pattern and a system that matches that pattern. The system is also matched by the pattern in Fig. 10, but the RAR in Fig. 10 must match all three repositories and one or more tasks that connect them.

Fig. 10. Central repository pattern and an example matched system

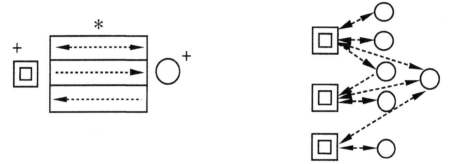

Fig. 11. Distributed repository pattern and example matched system

These repetition operators provide parallel repetition in the patterns. That is, the repetition of elements connected to the same element or group of elements. Two examples of parallel repetition are multiple streams between two filters, and multiple transaction programs accessing a single database. Recursive repetition involves an element that will connect, in turn, to the elements generated by the pattern. An example would be the pattern for a pipe and filter system. The next section describes a method to specify recursive patterns.

3.3 Grammar Productions

To handle recursive repetition, we extend the pattern mechanism to provide the equivalent of context free graph grammars. This is done using a limited version of graph grammars [FahBlo92]. The full power of unrestricted graph grammars is not required for specifying the patterns we are interested in.

As with all grammars, the rules have a left and right hand side. The left-hand side can be a non–terminal node or edge. It includes a context for the new non–terminal symbol that consists of primitive elements. The context is the interface of any system that can be generated using that grammar production. The right-hand side is a system graph with the same context as the left-hand side. When more than one element of the context is of the same type and has the same attributes, then the context elements must be labelled.

We have introduced two new visual symbols to represent non-terminals. The first is a rounded rectangle and is used to represent non-terminal nodes. The other is a wide arrow that is used to represent non-terminal edges. The non-terminals are labelled to distinguish them.

When a production is applied to a non-terminal node, only the ends of the connectors connected to the non-terminal node are changed (to the new nodes introduced by the production). The other ends of the connections remain connected to the same nodes.

As with conventional grammars, more than one rule may be provided for a given non-terminal. The same non-terminal node may be defined for more than one context. However, only those productions which have the same context as the non-terminal node may be applied.

Although the capabilities of the regular expression operators may be provided by the grammar mechanism, we believe that they provide a concise means of representing some structures. The grammar version of the structures would not be as clear. Instead, we define how the regular expression operators and grammar constructs interact.

The system matched by applying the '?', '+' or '*' operators a non-terminal is equivalent to replicating the non-terminal before expanding it. That is, not all of the systems matched by the non-terminal must be matched by the same parse.

Figure 12 shows a pattern that matches pipe and filter systems with no feedback between the filters. In all of the grammars shown in this paper, the first non–terminal on the left is the goal symbol of the grammar. The pattern is a non-terminal that is used in two rules. These rules state that a pipe and filter system is a task with two multiple stream connections, or a task connected by a multiple stream connection to a pipe and filter system.

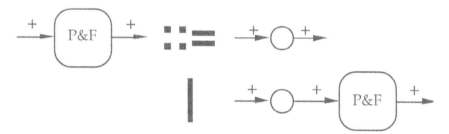

Fig. 12. Pipe and filter system with no feedback

A simple extension to the pipe and filter system is to allow feedback from one filter to a filter earlier in the pipeline. To do this, the system generated by a non-terminal must be able to communicate with all of the symbols generated previously. If a connection from the non-terminal is restricted to connecting to a single element in the rest of the pattern, we would require an infinite number of non-terminals, each with an additional connection in the context. Instead, we allow connections that have been modified by the '+' or '*' operator to be given more than once in the context in the right hand side, and in the context of the embedded symbol. Labels are used to identify the connections that have been replicated. Figure 13 shows the pattern for a pipe and filter system with feedback.

The labels are local to the rule and have no binding when determining which elements of the context of the embedded symbol correspond to the context elements of the next production to be applied. At present, there is no means of making that restriction. All possible bindings are tried when parsing the graph.

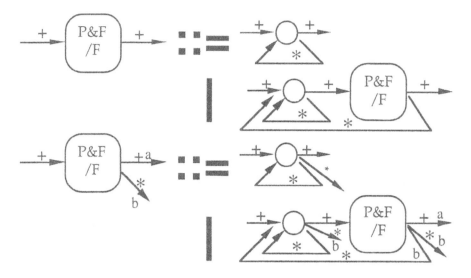

Fig. 13. Pipe and filter system with feedback

3.4 Strength of Pattern Match

Some systems may be matched by more than one pattern. For example, the pattern given in Fig. 13 not only matches a general pipe and filter system with feedback, but it also matches pipe and filter systems without feedback. If we modify the pattern, replacing all '*' operators by '+' operators, we get a pattern that matches pipe and filter systems that have feedback between all tasks. It is advantageous to have some metric of the strength of the match. The ideal definition of the strongest match is the pattern that matches the fewest systems, although it still might match an infinite number of systems. In this section we define an approximation.

Suppose we have two pattern systems that match a given target system. We start by defining a partial order between corresponding elements of the two patterns that match the same minor system of the target system. The partial order is defined based on how the elements have been modified by the regular expression operators, and the '!' operator. This relation, for which we use the '≤' symbol, is given in Fig. 14. For elements a of one pattern and b of another, a ≤ b, if b is a better match than a. The symbol '~' is used to represent an unmodified element and the symbol '○' is used to represent an element missing from the pattern. Since a partial order is transitive and reflexive, the transitive and reflexive closures of Fig. 14 are also defined. We extend the partial order from individual elements of the two patterns to the entire patterns in the obvious way. One pattern match is stronger than the other if the partial order holds for all elements of the two patterns.

$$* \; \leq \; +$$ $$* \; \leq \; !* \qquad !* \; \leq \; !+$$

$$+ \; \leq \; ? \qquad ? \; \leq \; !? \qquad !+ \; \leq \; !?$$

$$+ \; \leq \; {\sim} \qquad {\sim} \; \leq \; !{\sim} \qquad !+ \; \leq \; !{\sim}$$

$$? \; \leq \; \circ \qquad * \; \leq \; \circ$$

Fig. 14. Partial order for regular expressions

4. Taxonomy

The classes of our taxonomy are motivated from two sources, Mary Shaw's paper on higher level abstractions [Shaw89] and the book *Coordinated Systems* [FilFri84]. It currently contains 5 classes, 2 of which have several subclasses. Some of these patterns have already been shown in figures. Figure 15 gives an outline of the taxonomy.

Class	*Notes*
Pipe and Filter	
Unidirectional	
Without Feedback	
Simple	Fig. 12
With Feedback	Fig. 13
Non-overlapping Feedback	
Bidirectional	
Simple	
Random Repository	
Central	Fig. 10
Layered	
Distributed	Fig. 11
Message Network	
Layered	Fig. 16
Knowledge Interpreter	Fig. 7, connectors modified by
'+'	
Client–Server	Fig. 10, RAR replaced by a Task

Fig. 15. Taxonomy outline

The pipe and filter system with non-overlapping feedback is similar to that with general feedback, but the feedback connectors may not overlap. They may be between successive sets of the filters, or nested. The bidirectional pipe and filter system is similar to the unidirectional case without feedback, but the streams may be bidirectional, or they may be unidirectional in either direction. The message network is a set of tasks that are connected by one or more message connectors. There are no restrictions on the number of message connectors, or the number of tasks.

The pattern for the layered system is shown in Fig. 16. It consists of two productions and is similar to the simple pipe and filter system. The difference is that the procedure call communication primitive is used, and the non-terminal node is replicated. The layered random repository pattern is similar to the pipe and filter pattern.

It may be described as a sequence of RARs where each RAR is connected to the next by one or more tasks and memory access connections.

The client server pattern is similar to the central repository pattern, but the central entity is a task instead of a RAR. The distinction between these two structures is impossible without the types provided by our notation or behavioural information for the central component.

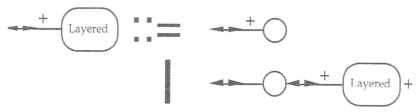

Fig. 16. Layered system pattern

5. Conclusions

It is currently not known if our pattern mechanism is sufficient to describe all of the interesting structure classes. It does, however, handle a reasonable number of them. We are a little concerned about controlling the complexity of the descriptions. The graph grammars necessary to describe some involved structures may not be easy to understand. This may simply be a consequence of a complex structure and any representation of the structure would be just as complex.

There are several reasons we believe this to be an appropriate representation for system structure. The first is that it uses a similar technique to that used to express language structure: regular expressions and context free grammars. It is essentially a graphical form of extended BNF notation. The second advantage of the notation is that it is easily expandable to include new primitive element types.

The notation provides a means for reasoning about system structure. It can be used to describe the structure of existing systems and of system designs. It may also provide a framework within which to express other system properties such as behaviour. One possible mechanism to express function or behaviour is to map each element of the system to a description in CSP [Hoare78] or CCS [Miln80]. This notation may prove useful in developing maintenance theories for large software systems.

The taxonomy provides a means of comparing system structure classes and a means of classifying the structure of existing systems. This information can used to build a syllabus of useful system structures that may be used when designing new systems. This syllabus should provide guidance in choosing a structure appropriate to the problem. Instead of emphasizing a single structure class, the designer may choose to use different structures in different parts of the system.

Some work has begun on an implementation of this technique. We have a Prolog representation of the notation, and it has been used in the development of predicates that check the validity of a system description, compute the interface of a system, and evaluate equivalence and specialization. These predicates are used to implement direct pattern matching and subpattern matching. We are working on an interface for the visual notation which will be able to interact with the Prolog engine.

Acknowledgements

We would like to thank Kevin Schneider for his assistance in proofreading this paper and Mary Shaw for her comments and insights.

References

[FahBlo92] Fahmy, H., Blostein, D., "A Survey of Graph Grammars: Theory and Applications", *11th International Conference on Pattern Recognition*, Sept. 1992.

[FilFri84] Fillman, R. E., Friedman, D. P., *Coordinated Computing: Tools and Techniques for Distributed Software*, McGraw-Hill, New York, 1984.

[Hoare78] Hoare, C. A. R., "Communicating Sequential Processes", *CACM*, Vol. 21, No. 8, Aug. 1978, pp. 666-677.

[Miln80] Milner, R., *A Calculus of Communicating Systems*, Lecture Notes in Computer Science 92, Springer-Verlag, New York, 1980.

[Shaw89] Shaw, M., "Larger Scale Systems Require Higher–Level Abstractions", *Proceedings of the Fifth International Workshop on Software Specification and Design*, IEEE Computer Society, 1989, pp. 143-146.

Regularities in Software Systems

Naftaly H. Minsky*

Department of Computer Science
Rutgers University
New Brunswick, NJ 08903 USA
minsky@cs.rutgers.edu

Abstract. Regularities, or the conformity to unifying principles, are essential to the comprehensibility, manageability and reliability of large software systems. Yet, as is argued in this paper, the inherent globality of regularities makes them very hard to establish in traditional methods, unless they are imposed on a system by some kind of higher authority. This paper explores an approach to regularities which greatly simplifies their implementation, making them more easily employable for taming of the complexities of large systems. This approach, which is based on the concept of law-governed architecture (LGA), provides system designers and builders with the means for establishing regularities simply by declaring them formally and explicitly as *the law of the system*. Once such a *law-governed regularity* is declared, it is enforced by the environment in which the system is developed. Although not all desirable regularities can be established this way, it is argued that the range of feasible "law-governed regularities," which can be easily defined and efficiently enforced, is sufficiently broad for this to become a powerful software engineering technique.

keywords: Complexity in software, regularities, software-development environments.

1 Introduction

In his classic paper "No Silver Bullet" [1], Brooks cites *complexity* as a major reason for the great difficulties we have with large software systems, arguing that "software entities are more complex for their size than perhaps any other human construct," and that their "complexity is an *inherent* and *irreducible* property of software systems" [emphasis mine]. Brooks explains this bleak assessment as follows: "The physicist labors on, in a firm faith that there are *unifying principles* to be found ... no such faith comforts the software engineer."

Brooks is surely right in viewing conformity to unifying principles, i.e., *regularities*, as essential to our ability to understand and manage large systems; but he is overly pessimistic about the role that regularities can play in software systems. It is true that one is not likely to find many *regularities of repetition* in software, because plain repetitions can be easily abstracted out and "made

---

* Work supported in part by NSF grant No. CCR-8807803

into a subroutine," in Brooks' words. But there are other, more subtle kinds of regularities, that may "comfort the software engineer," provided that they can be easily and reliably established.

The kind of regularity we have in mind here is any structural or behavioral *property that holds true for the entire system*, or, at least, for a significant, well defined part of it.[2] Examples of such regularities that simplify large systems and make them more manageable and more reliable can be found in many domains: The regular organization of the streets and avenues in the city of Manhattan greatly simplifies navigation in the city, and the planning of services for it; the protocol that all drivers use at intersections of roads makes driving so much easier and safer; and the layered organization of communication-networks provides a framework within which these systems can be constructed, managed and understood. In fact, a large system of any kind which has no regularities is necessarily incomprehensible, which means that regularities are quite indispensable for large systems in general.

But in spite of the great importance of regularities, and their promise for taming the complexity of systems, regularities are underutilized in software systems, and not sufficiently appreciated by software designers. This is probably because regularities are inherently hard to establish, unless they are imposed on a system by some kind of higher authority. The problem with regularities stems from their *intrinsic globality*. Unlike an algorithm or a data structure that can be built into few specific modules, a regularity is a principle that must be observed everywhere in the system, and thus cannot be localized by traditional methods. One can, of course, establish a desired regularity by painstakingly building all components of the system in accordance with it. But, as we shall see in this paper, such a "manual" implementation of regularities is laborious, unreliable, unstable and difficult to verify and to change. While certain regularities are usually imposed on a system by the programming languages in which it is written, languages do not, and, as we shall argue later, probably cannot, support a sufficiently wide range of regularities.

These difficulties can be alleviated, for a wide range of useful regularities, by means of a previously proposed Law-Governed Architecture (LGA) [10],[11]. Under this architecture a desired regularity can be established in a given system simply by declaring it formally and explicitly as *the law of the system*, to be *enforced* by the environment in which the system is developed. Besides the ease of establishing regularities under this architecture, the resulting *law-governed regularities* are much more reliable and more flexible then manually implemented ones.

The subject of this paper, and its main contribution, is not LGA (which has been described) but the potential impact of law-governed regularities on software engineering, and the range of such regularities that can be effectively established under LGA. We start, in Section 2, with a discussion of the nature of regularities in software, and with an analysis of their implementation difficulties. In Section

---

[2] We are using here the dictionary definition of the term "regular" as "conforming to a rule or a principle".

3 we provide a very brief overview of LGA, with a fairly detailed, but mostly informal, illustration of the manner in which regularities are established under this architecture; and the manner in which these regularities may evolve, and be refined, throughout the evolutionary lifetime of a system. Section 4 contains a sample of the type of regularities that can be effectively established under LGA, along with a brief discussion of the expected benefits of each of such regularities.

2 The Nature of Regularities, and their Implementation Difficulties

The term "regularity" refers in this paper to any *global* property of a system; that is, a property that holds true for every part of the system, or for some significant and well defined subset of its parts. Thus, the statement "class B inherits from class C," in some object-oriented system, does not express a regularity, since it concerns just two specific classes; but the statement "*every* class in the system inherits from C" does express a regularity, and so does the statement "*only* class B inherits from C," both of which employ universal quantification.

We already mentioned one well known example of a regularity in software, namely, the *layered organization* that partitions the modules of a system into groups called layers, asserting that a module can call only modules at its own layer or at the layer immediately below; we will return to this particular regularity in the following section. Another important regularity is *encapsulation* – the principle that no object in a system can penetrate the interior of another object. This regularity is the basis for meaningful modularization, and is thus vital for all large systems.

In addition to such almost universal regularities, a given system may benefit from a variety of regularities designed specifically for it. As an example of such a "special purpose" regularity, consider the following *token-based protocol* which might be employed by a distributed system S in order to ensure *mutual exclusion* with respect to a given operation O:

1. No process performs operation O unless it possesses a certain token T.
2. Initially, there is only one copy of T in the system.
3. Token T may be transferred from one process to another, but no process ever duplicates T.

Note that to be effective, this protocol must be a regularity; that is, it must be obeyed *everywhere* in the system, because the desired mutual exclusion would be endangered by any violation of this protocol, even by a single process.

The utility of regularities in large systems is almost self evident, but their implementation is very problematic. Conceptually the simplest, and currently the most common, technique for establishing regularities is to implemented them *manually*; that is, to carefully construct the system according to the desired regularities. The problems with this approach, which are due to the inherent globality of regularities, are exemplified by the following difficulties one would have with the above mentioned token-based regularity (or protocol), if it is to be implemented manually:

1. It would be very *difficult to carry out* this implementation, because it must be done painstakingly in many different parts of the system. It would, in particular, be difficult to ensure that *no* process in the system S ever performs operation O without possessing the token T, and that no extra copy of T is ever made, anywhere in the system.
2. Any *verification* (formal or informal) that a given system satisfies this protocol, involves the analysis of *all* (or, at least, many) parts of the system.
3. This protocol would be very *unstable* with respect to the evolution of the system. Indeed, even if we are able to ascertain that the protocol is satisfied by a given version of the system, we cannot have much confidence in its satisfiability in future versions. Because, due to the global nature of the protocol, it can be compromised by a change *anywhere in the system.*
4. Finally, this protocol would be very *difficult to change*, even if the change itself is small, because such a change would have to be introduced *manually* into many parts of the system. Changes spread out in this way are very expensive and notoriously prone to error.

Since these problems are quite clearly endemic to all manually implemented regularities, it follows that it would be much better for regularities to be *imposed* on a system by some kind of "higher authority".

Perhaps the most obvious such authority that can impose regularities on a system is the programming language in which this system is written. In fact, certain types of regularities are routinely imposed by various languages on the programs written in them. These include *block-structured* name scoping, *encapsulation, inheritance,* and various regularities involving *types.* In spite of the obvious importance of such built-in regularities, the imposition of regularities by means of a programming language has several serious limitations.

— Only very few types of regularities can be thus built into any given language; and a regularity built into the very fabric of a language tends to be rigid, and not easily adaptable to an applications at hand.
— Regularities that do not have universal applicability should not be built into a general purpose language.
— Programming languages usually adopt a *module-centered view* of software. They deal mostly with the internal structure of individual modules, and with the interface between pairs of directly interacting modules. But languages generally provide no means for making explicit statements about the system as a whole, and thus no means for specifying inter-module regularities beyond what is built into the language itself. There is, for example, no language known to the author that provide the means for imposing a layered structure on a system, although one can of course build such a structure manually.
— Language-imposed regularities are obviously not effective for multilingual systems, where regularities are particularly needed.

For all these reasons it follows that the imposition of regularities requires a software architecture that provide a global view of systems; such is our *law-governed architecture*.

3 An Overview of Law Governed Architecture (LGA)

The main novelty of law-governed architecture is that it associates with every software-development projects an *explicit* set of rules, called the *law* of the system, which is *enforced* by the environment in which the system is developed. The law governs the following, seemingly distinct, aspects of the project under its jurisdiction:

1. The structure of the system being developed.
2. The process of development and evolution of this system.
3. The evolution of the law itself.

This paper is concerned mostly with the first of the above roles of the law, i.e., with the imposition of regularities on the system. Yet, the broader, evolutionary, aspects of the law cannot be entirely ignored if we are to understand how regularities are established under LGA, and how they are refined and maintained throughout the evolutionary lifetime of a project. Such broader view of LGA is provided in this section, based on experience with Darwin, which is an experimental software-development environment that supports LGA[3].

Generally speaking, the law deals with the internal structure of the system being developed, not with its functionality. One can, for example, have a law that impose a layered structure on a system, quite independently of whatever it is that the system is doing. More specifically, the law governs the system under its jurisdiction by regulating the various interactions between its component-objects (say, modules) mostly ignoring the internal details of these objects. The interactions being regulated may be either *dynamic*, like the exchange of a message between pairs of objects, or *static*, like the existence of an inheritance relation between classes (in the case of an object-oriented language). The law, may, in particular, prescribe which objects can send which messages to which other objects; it may call for certain messages to be changed, or be rerouted to other than their nominal target; and it may prescribe some other actions to be carried out in conjunction with, or instead of, an attempted message. Such prescription, for a given interaction, is called the *ruling* of the law for this interaction.

The requirement that the law of a system must be strictly and efficiently enforced, means that we must restrict ourselves to very simple types of laws. Consequently, laws under LGA are *differential* rather than *integral*. That is, the ruling of the law concerning a given interaction, depends only on the nature of the interaction itself, and on its immediate context, and not on the effects that an interaction may end up having on the system at large. Thus, for example, the

---

[3] To be precise, this overview is of Darwin/2 [17], which is a major revision of the Darwin/1 environment described in [11].

law cannot state that there shall be mutual exclusion with respect to a given operation, but it is possible to design a differential law, such as the token-protocol of Section 2, which does ensure mutual-exclusion.

A software development project starts under LGA with the definition of the *initial law* that establishes the general framework within which the project is to operate and evolve. We will now consider an informal example of such an initial law, designed to support the development of *layered systems*. (For a formal expression of a very similar law, which has been actually used under Darwin, see [11].)

3.1 A Law of Layered Systems – a Case Study

The example-law presented in this section partitions the modules of the system, developed under a project P governed by this law, into groups called "layers". Using this grouping, the law imposes the well known *layered constraint* on the interaction between modules, as an *invariant of the evolution* of project P. Furthermore, this law provides for the controlled evolution of the law itself, allowing the manager of the project and its various programmers to refine the law in a carefully circumscribed manner, throughout the course of software development. In particular, the manager is authorized to impose arbitrary *prohibitions* on the interaction between modules, while each programmer is authorized to specify which messages are *acceptable* to his own modules, subject to the layered constraint, and to the manager's prohibitions.

This law is presented here, mostly informally, as consisting of four rules (enclosed in boxes) that govern four distinct aspects of the project under its jurisdiction. Only rule 3 is specified formally (for the sake of illustration) but without detailed explanation of the formalism itself, which is described in [13].

Rule 1 below determines the *structure of the object-base* that would support project P throughout its evolutionary lifetime.

rule 1 *The objects representing program-modules are partitioned into* layers; *the objects representing the builders of the system are partitioned into two roles:* manager *and* programmer; *and each module is designated as being* owned *by some programmer.*

Technically, these partitions are defined by certain attributes associated with the various objects populating this project. The semantics of the resulting groupings of these objects is defined, in effect, by the other rules in this law, as we shall see.

Rule 2 below governs the *process of development and evolution* under project P, by establishing the authority of the various builder-roles.

rule 2 *A* manager *can create programmer-objects, and a* programmer *can make modules, becoming the* owner *of each module he makes. The owner of a module can program it, set its level, remove it, and pass its ownership to some other programmer.*

This rule defines, in effect, what it means to be the *manager* of a project, and what it means to be an *owner* of a module. Note that the Darwin environment itself has no built-in concept of a "manager" or of "ownership," but, as we have just seen, it provides for such concepts to be established specifically for each project, by means of its law.

Rule 3 (which is specified *formally* below) governs the *structure of the system being developed*. It essentially states that a message M sent by S to T would be delivered to its destination only if the following three conditions are satisfied (for a detailed explanation of the structure of such rules see [13]): (a) the layered constraint; (b) this message is not *prohibited* (as defined by prohibited-rules, which, according to rule rule 4 below, can be written into the law only by the manager); and (c) this message is *acceptable* to the target module T (as defined by the acceptable-rules, which, according to rule 4 can be written into the law only by the owner of T).

```
rule 3      sent(S,M,T) :-  level(Ls)@S,level(Lt)@T,
                            Lt<= Ls <=Lt+1,
                            not prohibited(S,M,T),
                            acceptable(S,M,T),
                            $do(deliver(M)@T).
```

Finally, rule 4 below governs the *evolution of the law itself*, allowing the manager of the project, and the various programmers to refine the regularities of the system during its development.

rule 4 *The law can change* only *as specified below:*

1. *A manager can add to the law (and remove from it) arbitrary* prohibited-rules, *which, according to rule 3, serve as prohibitions.*
2. *Every programmer can add to the law (and remove from it)* acceptable-rules, *which, according to rule 3, define which messages are acceptable to to any of* his *own modules, and which objects can send these messages.*

Note that this particular law, which is, of course, merely an example of what can be done under LGA, establishes a framework which is analogous to, but much more general than, the conventional *module-interconnection frameworks* (MIFs) which are based on *selective export*, as in Eiffel in particular. The analogy comes from an apparent similarity between Eiffel's *export statements*, and our *acceptable*-rules. Both are anchored on a module, defining the kind of messages that can be sent to it.[4] Yet, our example-law has several characteristics which are unmatched by Eiffel, or by any conventional MIF known to the author.

First, under this law the layered-constraint is an *invariant of the evolution of this project* – unchangeable even by its manager. Our ability to establish such

---

[4] While the export-statement must be included textually within a module, our acceptable-rules are writable by the owner of the module they are anchored on – not a major difference.

invariants of evolution, without them being hard-wired into the environment, or into the language at hand, can attest to the power of this architecture.

Second, using `prohibition`-rules the manager can establish additional regularities, over the entire system. For example, the manager may prohibit modules designated as `tested` from calling untested ones.

Finally, even our `acceptable`-rules are significantly more general than the export-statements. The Eiffel's export-statements in a given module m list explicitly the *names* of the modules that can send a given message to m (unless it is a universal export). In our case, on the other hand, the analogous specification, by means of the `acceptable`-rules, can be by some condition defined over the attributes of the various modules of the system. These allows programmers to formulate *general prescriptive policies*, concerning the use of their modules. Here are two, informally stated, examples of policies concerning a given module m that can be expressed by means of a single `acceptable`-rule writable by the programmer of m.

— Module m can accept messages from *every* module at the layer of m.
— Module m can accept a specified message from *every module owned by a programmer Jones*.

3.2 Law Enforcement and the Implementation of Darwin

space limitations rule out any detailed discussion of the law-enforcement mechanism of LGA. Here we provide only a very brief overview of this mechanism, as it is currently used in Darwin for the Eiffel language, and as it is planned for C++. This is followed with an overview of the Darwin environment itself.

When a new module is introduced into a given project (or when an existing one is modified) it is examined for consistency with the law, with one of the following consequences:

1. The module may be found to be completely consistent with the law, and be admitted into the project without any change.
2. The text of the module may be modified according to the rulings of the law. Such modifications may, in particular, be used to perform run-time validity checks, which cannot be resolved statically.
3. The module may be found to be definitely in violation of the law, and be rejected by the enforcer.

Thus, the law enforcer in Darwin simply does not allow the creation of programs that would violate the law. As an indication of the types of laws that can be handled this way we point out that the laws defining the various regularities discussed in this paper are currently enforceable under Darwin, and mostly without any run-time overhead. Run-time validation is, however, required for most token-based regularities discussed in Section 4.2.

Structurally, the Darwin environment has essentially two levels: (1) the *abstract*, language-independent, level that maintains an object-base of the project, defines the concept of law, and provides a framework for its enforcement; and (2) the *concrete* level that contains a set of *language interfaces*, one for each programming language which may be used by any of the modules of the system. Currently, Darwin has interfaces for two, very different, languages: an interface called LGA/Prolog, for the logic-programming language Prolog [3]; and an interface called LGA/Eiffel for the object-oriented language Eiffel [7]; and an interface for C++ is being planned.

A *language-interface*, for a given language, performs two functions. First, it maps the abstract concepts of this architecture, such as *object* and *interaction* between objects, to certain concrete constructs of the language at hand. For example, our Eiffel-interface maps the abstract concept of objects in Darwin to Eiffel-classes, and it maps the abstract concept of interaction to procedure-calls that cross class-boundary, and to various static relationships between classes, such as inheritance and redefinition. The second function of a language-interface in Darwin is to provide the language specific part of the law-enforcer.

4 A Sample of Law-Governed Regularities

In this section we sample from a wide range of law-governed regularities which should be useful for large systems. The regularities to be discussed here are not new *per se*. Some of these regularities have been incorporated into certain conventional languages; others have been formulated by the designers of specific systems, to be programmed "manually" into these systems; and still others have been formulated by programming-managers as methodologies to be employed by their programmers. What is new here is that under LGA, all these different regularities can be, and have been, formulated explicitly and formally as laws, and then efficiently enforced by the environment in which the system is developed. Such regularities are easier to establish and to change, and are far more reliable, then the manually implemented ones.

It should be pointed out that this sample of regularities is far from complete. In particular, regularities in distributed systems, such as the token-based protocol discussed above, are mentioned only very briefly here. However, such regularities are discussed in detail in [9],[6].

4.1 Regulating the Use of the Unsafe Primitives of a Language

Every practical programming language has some *unsafe* primitive features whose careless use may have disastrous consequences. The use of many of these features, which are often called "harmful", can be carefully regulated under LGA, helping to make systems more reliable, safer, and in a sense simpler.

A familiar example of an unsafe feature of a language is the *dispose* primitive of Pascal, which, if used carelessly, may cause the phenomenon of *dangling reference* with its quite unpredictable consequences for the entire system. Additional examples of unsafe features which are common in languages include *address arithmetic*, and certain *type conversions*. Careless use of any of these features, and of others like them, can violate the semantics of the host language. In particular, the many unsafe features of C++ may allow any object to manipulate the private space of other objects, thus violating the principle of *encapsulation* – perhaps the most important regularity of object-oriented programming.

Certain features of a language may be considered unsafe even if they do not violate the semantics of the language. For example, in a patient-monitoring system, access to the actuators that control the flow of various fluids and gases into the body of a patient is clearly unsafe, as it is crucial to the life of this patient. More generally, in *embedded systems*, the ability to operate on the outside world (typically represented by system-calls) is often similarly unsafe.

The worth of regulation over the use of unsafe primitives can be demonstrated by the kernel-based architecture of operating systems. The *kernel* is a small part of the system which presents the rest of it with several fundamental abstractions such as that of a *process* and of *virtual-memory* which, if the kernel is written correctly, are invariant of whatever is done outside the kernel. This architecture is made possible by the *confinement* to the kernel of certain unsafe capabilities provided by the bare machine, such as the ability to interrupt the CPU, and the unrestricted access to the main memory. This confinement to the kernel is a regularity, in our sense of this term, because it is a *universal statement* about the system. Namely, that no part of the system except the kernel can use the unsafe primitives in question.

The need for such confinement is not restricted to operating systems, of course. It would, for example, be invaluable for the above mentioned patient-monitoring system, which can be made much safer if access to the various critical actuators is *confined* to few specific modules that are supposed to manage them. And C++ programs, in general, can be made much more reliable, and easier to debug, if the various unsafe features of this language are confined to the regions of the program that really need them, while the rest of the system is subject to the much stricter object-oriented discipline.

Unfortunately, with few notable exceptions, programming languages generally do not provide any means for regulating the use of the unsafe primitives built into the language itself. And the special hardware that supports confinement in operating systems is not available for use inside user-programs outside the kernel.

One of the few languages that does allow for some regulation over its unsafe features is Modula-3 [2]. This language explicitly characterizes certain of its primitive features as unsafe, allowing them to be used only inside modules that are explicitly declared to be "unsafe". This is a step in the right direction, but it does not go far enough. It should, in particular, be possible to regulate the various unsafe features of a language *individually*, by, for instance, confining each to a different module. It should also be useful to regulate the interaction of such "unsafe modules" with the rest of the system, and to regulate the construction and evolution of such modules. Such flexible controls, and others, are possible under LGA.

Under LGA/Eiffel, in particular, the law governs the ability of an Eiffel-class to have procedures written in C – the main unsafe feature of the Eiffel language. Thus, one can confine the use of C to certain classes, or to certain types of classes – say, classes written by a certain group of programmers, or classes residing in the lowest layer of the system. Moreover, one can regulate the interaction of classes that use C with the rest of the system. For example, only certain classes may be allowed to inherit from classes that use C. Many other unsafe features would be subject to control under the planned LGA/C++ interface.

4.2   Token-based Regularities

Many useful structures and control mechanisms are based on the notion of a *token* – an item that, by its dictionary definition [18], "tangibly signifies authority and authenticity". Such, for example, is the mutual exclusion protocol discussed in the introduction, where the movable but unique token T represents the exclusive authority to perform operation O. Another example is the well known *capability-based* access control mechanism [4], under which operations on objects are authorized by tokens called "capabilities". There are also many real-life processes which are regulated by tokens. For example, entry into theaters is regulated by means of tokens called *theater-tickets*; the financial activities of our society are largely regulated by tokens called *dollars*; and access to roads is regulated by means of tokens called "tokens". These and other real-life token-controlled processes have close analogies in computer systems, and are themselves often subject to computer support.

The great virtue of token-based control is that the validity of an operation can be determined strictly *locally*, on the basis of the token being presented. But this locality depends on the existence of some underlying global regularities. Specifically, for an item T to serve as a token in a given system, conferring on its holder the power to perform a certain operation O, the system must satisfy two kinds of regularities: First, it must be *impossible* to perform O without possessing T; and second, the *creation and distribution of T-items must be strictly controlled*, so that the mere possession of a token can be taken as *prima facie* proof of the authority it is supposed to represent. Unfortunately, these, like other kinds of regularities, are impossible to establish reliably unless they are imposed on the system by some higher authority. This is particularly true for distributed systems where the management of tokens cannot be centralized. (We note here that while cryptographic techniques can be used in many cases to ensure the *authenticity* of tokens, they are often not very helpful in providing tokens the *exclusive authority* which make them meaningful.)

Most programming languages give no support for token-based regularities, since languages generally provide for almost no control over the creation of objects, and over the transfer of objects (or of pointers to objects) ¿from one part of a program to another. While some specific token-based regularities have been built into certain computational platforms (like operating system [4]), and into some programming languages [22], none of them provides the means for establishing a broad spectrum of such regularities, of the kind described below. Consequently, if a certain token-based regularity is desired in a given system, it would usually have to be implemented manually, with all the disadvantages of such an implementation.

Under LGA, on the other hand, it is possible to establish a wide range of token-based regularities simply by means of appropriate laws. The range of regularities that can be supported under LGA span several dimensions, such as:

- **The nature of the authority represented by a token:** In particular, a token may represent the right, or power, to operate in a certain way on a single object, as in the case of a *capability*; or, in some analogy to a master-key, a token may provide the power to operate on a whole set of objects.
- **The manner in which a token itself is affected by the operation which it is used to authorize:** In particular, the token may be completely unaffected by its use, and thus be usable an indefinite number of times; it may be usable just once; or some specified number of times.
- **The controlled means provided for the creation of tokens, and for their distribution:** For example, the ability to move a token from one object to another may be conditioned on the availability of certain other tokens, as proposed in [5],[8]. Also, tokens may be allowed to be copied, or just be moved from one place to another.

Several examples of laws that impose various types of token-based regularities under LGA are discussed in [10] and in [12].

4.3 Monitoring

There are many situations in which one would like to monitor a certain kind of messages by notifying a given object (the "monitor") of their occurrence. Such monitoring can be useful for debugging; it may help in fine tuning a system by collecting statistics about various interactions between its parts; it may be used to provide various parts of a system with information about the activity of other parts, as it is done in the GARDEN system [19]; it may help in the defense against viruses and other attacks on a system; and it may facilitate on-line auditing of financial systems.

A specific monitoring regime is often a regularity, in the sense that it requires a certain protocol to be observed by many different parts of the system, and it is, therefore, difficult to implement manually. Moreover, there is a wide range of possible monitoring regimes, not all of which are likely be built into any one programming language or environment. In particular, monitoring regimes may differ along the following dimensions: (a) the nature of messages to be monitored, and the circumstances under which they should be monitored; (b) the identity of the monitor; (c) the actions that should be carried out when a message to be monitored occurs; and (d) the mechanisms for starting and stopping a monitoring activity. Many such regimes can be effectively established by law under LGA, and several of them have been experimentally implemented under Darwin.

4.4 Regularities in Object-Oriented Systems

In a series of previous papers [15, 20, 21, 16] we have shown that most of the fundamental structures of object-oriented programming, including *inheritance* and *delegation*, and many variations of these structures, are regularities that can be established under LGA by means of explicit laws. While the resulting flexibility should be highly beneficial for exploratory programming, most *object-oriented systems* are likely to be built in conventional object-oriented languages, such as C++ or Eiffel, which support some fixed concepts of inheritance, and of related structures. In this section we discuss some of the law-governed regularities which are likely to be useful for systems written in one of these conventional object-oriented languages.

First, the various types of regularities discussed so far in this paper are applicable to OO-systems, just as to any other kind of systems. In particular, it is often useful to group the classes of an OO-system into various clusters, by associating appropriate attributes with the objects that represents these classes in the object-base of Darwin. Such a partition can then serve as a basis for various regularities, as we have done for layered systems in Section 3. Also, the regulation of unsafe features may be very beneficial for OO-systems, particularly for systems written in C++, which has a lot of very unsafe features to regulate. Token-based and monitoring regularities should also be useful for OO-systems.

In addition, the special structures of OO-systems require special regulations. In particular, one may want to regulate which classes *can*, or *must*, inherit from which other classes. Also, one may want to establish the permissible relationships between a parent and its heirs, e.g., which aspects of the parent can be *visible* to, *redefined* by, or renamed by which of its heirs. For farther discussion of such regularities, and their motivation, the reader is referred to [14], which is based on our work with the LGA/Eiffel interface. In the following sub-section we present a detailed example that motivates some of these, and some other regularities in OO-systems.

An Example: Creating a Killable Class of Objects Consider a system built in an OO-language such as Eiffel, that provides garbage collection. It is well known that in such a language it is impossible to explicitly remove an object, because there may be references to it anywhere in the system. Given this, suppose that we would like to create a class C of objects that are *killable* in the following sense. A message `kill` sent to a C-object x should have the effect specified below (where by the term C-object we mean an instance of class C, or of any class that inherits directly or indirectly from C.)

1. A certain "burial procedure" B should be carried out on x.
2. Any subsequent attempt to send any message to the "killed" object x, *from anywhere* in the system, should result in a certain *error response* E.

Now, it turns out that it is impossible to ensure such behavior for all C-objects, without building it manually in many parts of the system. About the best we can do in Eiffel is the following:

1. Build into class C a boolean attribute `alive` whose initial value is true, and a method `kill`, programmed to set the attribute `alive` to false, and to perform the required burial procedure B.
2. Make sure that the method `kill` cannot be redefined by **any** class that inherits (directly or indirectly) from C.
3. Have *all* methods of class C, and of *any* direct or indirect heir of C perform the error response, E if applied to an object that has been killed.

Part (a) of this implementation is localized, in the class C, and is thus easy to accomplish. The other two parts, however, are regularities which must be satisfied in many parts of the system. It so happens that the regularity (b) above is supported by Eiffel, which allows a feature of a class to be declared as *frozen*, preventing it from being redefined by any heir of this class. But regularity (c) must be carried out manually, by programming in the specified manner *all* methods of *all* the classes that inherit directly or indirectly from C – a potentially difficult, and highly unreliable proposition. Thus, Eiffel provides us with no assistance in establishing this kind of regularity, nor does any other object-oriented language. Under LGA/Eiffel, on the other hand, the problematic regularity (c) above can be easily imposed by the law of the system.

5 Conclusion

In his book Symmetries and Reflections, the theoretical Physicist Eugene Wigner wrote [23]:

> "Physics does not endeavor to explain nature. In fact, the great success of physics is due to a restriction of its objectives: it only endeavors to explain the *regularities* in the behavior of objects".

Software engineering should, perhaps, similarly focus on the formalization of regularities, and on understanding their role in software systems. This paper is a step in that direction.

References

1. Frederick P. Jr. Brooks. No silver bullet – the essence and accidents of software engineering. *IEEE Computer*, pages 10–19, April 1987.
2. L. Cardelli, J. Dinahue, L. Glassman, M. Kalsow Jordan, B., and G. Nelson. Modula-3 report (revised). Technical Report 52, Digital System Research Center, November 1989.
3. W.F. Clocksin and C.S. Mellish. *Programming in Prolog*. Springer-Verlag, 1981.
4. P.J. Denning. Fault tolerant operating systems. *Computing Surveys*, 8(4):359–389, December 1976.
5. M. A. Harrison, W. L. Ruzzo, and J. D. Ullman. Protection in operating systems. *Communications of the ACM*, 19(8):461–471, Aug. 1976.
6. J. Leichter and N.H. Minsky. Obligations in law-governed distributed systems. Technical report, Rutgers University, LCSR, 1993. (In preperation).

7. B. Meyer. *Object-Oriented Software Construction*. Prentice-Hall, 1987.

8. N.H. Minsky. Selective and locally controlled transport of privileges. *ACM Transactions on Programming Languages and Systems (TOPLAS)*, 6(4):573–602, October 1984.

9. N.H. Minsky. Governing distributed systems: From protocols to laws. In *Proceedings of the Hawaii International Conference on System Sciences*, January 1991.

10. N.H. Minsky. The imposition of protocols over open distributed systems. *IEEE Transactions on Software Engineering*, February 1991.

11. N.H. Minsky. Law-governed systems. *The IEE Software Engineering Journal*, September 1991.

12. N.H. Minsky. Regularities in software systems. Technical Report LCSR-TR-204, Rutgers University, LCSR, April 1993.

13. N.H. Minsky. Law-governed regularities in software systems. Technical Report LCSR-TR-220, Rutgers University, LCSR, January 1994.

14. N.H. Minsky and P Pal. Establishing regularity in object-oriented (eiffel) systems. Technical Report LCSR-TR-227, Rutgers University, LCSR, June 1994. (Presented at the ECOOP Workshop on Patterns on OO programming, Bologna, July 1994).

15. N.H. Minsky and D. Rozenshtein. Law-based approach to object-oriented programming. In *Proceedings of the OOPSLA'87 Conference*, pages 482–493, October 1987.

16. N.H. Minsky and D Rozenshtein. Controllable delegation: An exercise in law-governed systems. In *Proceedings of the OOPSLA'89 Conference*, pages 371–380, October 1989.

17. N.H. Minsky and D. Rozenshtein. Specifications of the darwin/2 environment. Technical report, Rutgers University, LCSR, 1991.

18. W. Morris. *The American Heritage Dictionary of the English Language*. Houghton Mifflin Company, 1981.

19. S.P. Reiss. Working on the garden environment for conceptual programming. *IEEE Software*, 6(4):16–27, November 1987.

20. D. Rozenshtein and N.H. Minsky. Constraining interactions between objects in the presence of class inheritance. In *Proceedings of the 2nd International Workshop on Computer-Aided Software Engineering*, July 1988.

21. D. Rozenshtein and N.H. Minsky. Law-governed object-oriented system. *Journal of Object-Oriented Programming*, 1(6):14–29, March/April 1989.

22. R.E. Strom. Mechanism for compile-time enforcement of security. In *Proceedings of the ACM Symposium on Principles of Programming Languages*, pages 276–284, January 1983.

23. E. P. Wigner. *Symmetries and Reflections*. Ox Bow Press, 1979.

Formal Approaches to Software Architecture

David Garlan

School of Computer Science
Carnegie Mellon University
Pittsburgh, PA 15213, USA

Abstract. An important goal in software engineering is to describe complex software systems at an architectural level of abstraction. While good software engineers routinely employ architectural concepts in their designs these concepts are typically used idiomatically and in an ad hoc fashion. What appears to be missing is a formal basis for software architecture. But what exactly does this mean? In this paper we illustrate by example three approaches to formalizing software architecture. The first represents an industrial development effort to formalize a specific class of applications. The second shows how to use formalism to understand the design space for a commonly used architectural style. The third considers the problem of providing a formal basis for the generic notion of architectural interconnection.

1   Introduction

An important goal in software engineering is to describe complex software systems at an architectural level of abstraction. At this level the overall system structure becomes the important issue – gross organization, global control, intercomponent communication, etc. Good architectural design has always been a major factor in determining the success of a software system. However, while there are many useful architectural paradigms (pipelines, layered systems, client-server organizations etc.), they are typically understood only in an idiomatic way and applied in an ad hoc fashion. Consequently, software system designers have been unable to fully exploit commonalities in system architectures, make principled choices among design alternatives, specialize general paradigms to specific domains, or teach their craft to others.

What appears to be missing is a formal basis for software architecture. But what exactly does this mean? In this paper we illustrate three approaches to formalizing software architecture. The first represents an industrial development effort to formalize the architecture for a specific system. The second shows how to use formalism to understand the design space for an architectural style. The third considers the problem of providing a formal basis for architectural interconnection. We describe the advantages of each approach to show how complementary formalisms can provide a more complete understanding of software architecture than any one formalism alone.

2   The Value of Architectural Formalism

It is generally agreed that the existence of formal models and techniques for formal analysis are cornerstones of any true engineering discipline. But engineering disciplines use formalism in many different ways. Formalisms can be used to provide precise, abstract models. They can be used to provide analytical techniques based on these models. They can be used to provide notations for describing specific engineering designs. They can used to simulate behavior.

It is reasonable to expect that there will likewise be a wide variety of uses for formalism in the area of software architecture. Indeed, we can enumerate a number of distinct things that might be formalized, including:

1. **The architecture of a specific system.** Formalisms of this kind allow the software architect to describe a particular system to be built. Such formalisms can become part of the specification of the system, augmenting the use of informal characterizations of the system's architecture.
2. **An architectural framework – or architectural style.** Formalisms of this kind can be used to describe a common architectural abstraction for a family of systems. At one extreme are domain-specific reference architectures that represent a narrow product family. At another extreme are generic architectural patterns and idioms, which may cross many product families.
3. **A theory of software architecture.** Formalisms of this kind can be used to clarify the meaning of generic architectural concepts, such as architectural connection, hierarchical architectural representation, and architectural style. Additionally such formalisms can provide deductive a basis for analyzing systems at an architectural level. For example, such a theory might provide rules for determining when an architectural description is well-formed.
4. **The relationship between different architectures.** Formalisms of this kind can be used to elucidate a portion of the architectural space by showing how different architectures can be treated as specializations of a common abstraction.
5. **Formal semantics for architectural description languages.** This kind of formalism treats architectural description as a language issue and applies traditional techniques for representing semantics of languages.

Simply recognizing that many purposes may be served by architectural formalisms does not, of course, provide much guidance in carrying out these different kinds of formalization or in contrasting their relative benefits. To help clarify these issues we outline three examples that illustrate the categories outlined above.

3   Formalizing the Architecture of a Specific System

Many software systems start with an architectural design. These are typically described informally, since the abstractions at this level of design may have no direct means of expression in common notations for describing the structure of a software system. Module interconnection languages and modularization facilities of programming languages are often inadequate because they require the system designer to translate architectural abstractions into low-level primitives provided by the programming language [SG93, Sha93, AG94a]. Other notations may be appropriate for special kinds of architectural decomposition (e.g., object-oriented architectures), but may not apply to other situations and, again, may force the designer to use a lower level of abstraction than is appropriate.

To address this problem it is possible to describe the architecture of a specific system using a formal specification language. To illustrate how this can be done consider a formal architectural specification of an oscilloscope developed at Tektronix, Inc. [DG90]. Digital oscilloscopes and many other instrumentation systems are currently implemented by complex software systems, often involving multiple processors, sophisticated user interfaces, and an interface to external computing networks. A significant challenge in designing these systems is to find software organizations that permit rapid internal reconfiguration, exploitation of advanced signal processing hardware and software, and flexible interactions with a user interface.

The architectural framework developed to meet these requirements is one that decomposes the overall processing of an instrumentation system into a graph of transformations. Signals enter the system at one end, pass through a network of transformations and emerge as pictures and measurements that are displayed to the user on the front panel of the instrument. In this respect, the system can be viewed as a dataflow architecture. However, in addition to processing data, each of the individual transformers has an interface that allows the user to tune the transformation by configuring it through parameter settings. For example, the transformation that determines how a waveform is displayed on a screen is parameterized by scaling and positioning factors that allow the user to shrink, contract, and translate the waveform.

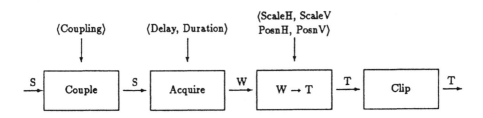

Fig. 1. An Acquisition Channel of an Oscilloscope

To describe the architecture of a specific instrumentation system one must to say what each of the component transformations is and how they are interconnected. Figure 1 shows how a small portion of an oscilloscope might be represented pictorially. To formalize this we begin by characterizing the data that is manipulated by the system. (We use the Z specification language [Spi89].) We model signals, waveforms, and traces as functions over the primitive domains of time, volts, and screen coordinates. Signals represent the inputs to the oscilloscope, waveforms the data as it is stored internally, and traces the pictures shown to a user.

$$Signal == AbsTime \longrightarrow Volts$$
$$Waveform == AbsTime \nrightarrow Volts$$
$$Trace == Horiz \nrightarrow Vert$$

For each of the components (represented by boxes in Figure 1) we provide a formal description that explains what are the configuration parameters, and for each configuration, what function is computed by the resulting transformer. To illustrate, consider the specification for the first component, called *Couple*. This transformer is used to subtract a DC offset from a signal. In this case the user has three choices of parameterization: DC, AC, and Ground. A choice of 'DC' leaves the signal unchanged; 'AC' subtracts the appropriate DC offset; 'GND' produces a signal whose value is zero volts at all times. The transformer can be modelled formally as a higher-order function: the first parameter (of type *Coupling*) determines what the resulting function (of type *Signal* $\longrightarrow$ *Signal*) will be.

$$Coupling ::= DC \mid AC \mid GND$$

$$Couple : Coupling \longrightarrow Signal \longrightarrow Signal$$

$$Couple\ DC\ s = s$$
$$Couple\ AC\ s = (\lambda t : AbsTime \bullet s(t) - dc(s))$$
$$Couple\ GND\ s = (\lambda t : AbsTime \bullet 0)$$

A *Waveform* is obtained from a *Signal* by extracting a time slice. The waveform is identical to the signal, except that it is defined only over a bounded interval. That interval is determined by three things: a reference time, called a trigger event, and two other relative time values, called delay and duration. The duration determines the length of the interval, while the delay determines when the interval is sampled relative to the trigger event. Again, we can use a higher-order function to model this component.

$$TriggerEvent == RelTime$$

$$Acquire : RelTime \times RelTime \longrightarrow TriggerEvent \longrightarrow Signal \longrightarrow Waveform$$

$$Acquire\ (delay, dur)\ trig\ s =$$
$$\{\ t : AbsTime \mid trig + delay \leq t \leq trig + delay + dur\ \} \lhd s$$

The other components of the architecture can be described similarly. (Details can be found in [DG90, GD90].) However, we are not finished, since we still have to show how the pieces are put together. To do this we interpret the connectors of the architecture as establishing an input/output relationship between the components. Then we collect the individual components and compose them into a single subsystem. As a first step, we package together the parameters of the individual components: these become the collective parameters of the subsystem as a whole. The subsystem itself is then defined as the functional composition of the individual transformers.

$$
\begin{array}{|l}
\hline
\text{\textit{ChannelParameters}} \rule[-0.3em]{0pt}{1em} \\
\quad c : Coupling \\
\quad delay, dur : RelTime \\
\quad scaleH : RelTime \\
\quad scaleV : Volts \\
\quad posnV : Vert \\
\quad posnH : Horiz \\
\hline
\end{array}
$$

$$
\begin{array}{|l}
ChannelConfiguration : ChannelParameters \longrightarrow TriggerEvent \longrightarrow Signal \longrightarrow Trace \\
\hline
ChannelConfiguration\ p = (\lambda\ trig : TriggerEvent\ \bullet \\
\quad Clip \circ WaveformToTrace(p.scaleH, p.scaleV, p.posnH, p.posnV) \\
\quad \circ Acquire(p.delay, p.dur)\ trig \circ Couple\ p.c)
\end{array}
$$

What has been gained by doing this? First, we have given a precise characterization of the system to be built. In this case the specification has been simplified considerably, but more realistic functions and configurations could have been defined. Second, and more importantly, we have exposed the architecture of the system as a configuration of components (here, parameterized data transformers) connected functionally through inputs and outputs.

4 Formalizing an Architectural Style

One of the difficulties in working with software architecture is that different designers may interpret an architectural idiom in different ways. For example, although two designers may both claim that their systems are built around a client-server paradigm, they may mean quite different things by that term [Ber92]. A related problem is that several systems may be designed with similar architectural structure, but the designers never recognize that these relationships exist. Consequently they miss opportunities to capitalize on the experience of other designers.

An architectural formalism can make relationships between architectures precise. To illustrate this, consider the problem of relating different systems built around the architectural paradigm of "implicit invocation." Implicit invocation systems are typically designed as systems in which components can "announce" events. Other components can register to receive announced events by associating a procedure with the event. When an event is announced all procedures associated with it will be invoked automatically by the system. In this way an event announcement causes the "implicit" invocation of the components that have registered for the event.

This simple description leaves many questions unanswered. What is the vocabulary of events? How is it determined? Can event announcements carry associated data? What is the level of concurrency in the handling of events? Different answers to these questions will lead to implicit invocation architectures with quite different properties [NGGS93].

One way to formalize these relationships is to start with the simple architectural abstraction outlined above, and then show how specific systems refine that abstraction. We can do this as follows: We begin by assuming there exist basic sets of events, methods, and component names. An architectural component can then be modelled (again using Z) as an entity that has a name and an interface consisting of a set of *methods* and a set of *events*.

$[EVENT, METHOD, CNAME]$

Component
name : $CNAME$
methods : $\mathbf{P}\ METHOD$
events : $\mathbf{P}\ EVENT$

A particular event (or method) is identified by a pair consisting of the name of a component and the event (or method) itself. In this way we can talk about the same event or method appearing in different components. We use the type abbreviations *Event* and *Method* to refer to these pairs (respectively).

$Event == CNAME \times EVENT$
$Method == CNAME \times METHOD$

An event system, *EventSystem*, consists of a set of components and an event manager. The event manager, *EM*, is a relation that associates events with methods that should be invoked when that event is announced.

EventSystem
components : $\mathbf{P}\ Component$
EM : $Event \leftrightarrow Method$

$\forall c_1, c_2 : components \bullet (c_1.name = c_2.name) \Leftrightarrow (c_1 = c_2)$
dom $EM \subseteq Events\ components$
ran $EM \subseteq Methods\ components$

The invariant of *EventSystem* asserts that the components in the system have unique names, and that the event manager contains only events and methods that actually exist in the system.

This characterization of *EM* is an extremely general one. In particular, this model allows the same event to be associated with many different methods, and even with many methods in the same component. It also permits some events to be associated with no methods. Further, it leaves open the issue of what components can announce events, and whether there are any restrictions on the methods that can be associated with those events. (For further details about this model see [GN91].)

We can now specialize this model to obtain the architectural paradigms for a number of specific systems. To illustrate, consider the implicit invocation mechanism that supports the Smalltalk-80 Model-View-Controller (MVC) paradigm [KP88]. This mechanism is based on the notion that any object can register as a "dependent" of any other object. When an object announces the "changed" event, the "update" method is implicitly invoked in each of its dependents. Thus, viewed as an implicit invocation system, the MVC provides a fixed, predetermined set of events (namely the "changed" event) and associated methods (namely the "update" method).

Formally, we first declare the *changed* event and *update* method to be elements of types *EVENT* and *METHOD*, respectively.

> changed : *EVENT*
> update : *METHOD*

We then model dependencies between objects as a relation between components. This dependency relation precisely determines the *EM* relation as follows: first, the events associated with each component is restricted to the set {*changed*}; and second, *EM* simply pairs *changed* events with the appropriate *update* methods.

─── *ST80* ───
EventSystem
dependents : *Component* ↔ *Component*
───────────────────────────────────
dom *dependents* ⊆ *components*
ran *dependents* ⊆ *components*
∀ c : *components* • c.events = {*changed*}
$EM = \{c_1, c_2 : components \mid (c_1, c_2) \in dependents \bullet$
$\quad\quad ((c_1.name, changed), (c_2.name, update))\}$
──

A consequence of these definitions is that each dependent in the system must have *update* as one its methods. We could formulate this as a simple lemma to be proved about such a system. In its implementation, Smalltalk-80 supports this obligation by providing a default *update* method in the Object class, which is inherited by all other classes in the system.

A quite different application of an implicit invocation architectural style is the tool integration mechanism of the Field System [Rei90]. In a Field environment tools communicate by "broadcasting" interesting events. Other tools can register patterns that indicate which events should be routed to them and which methods should be called when an event matches that pattern. When an event is announced, a pattern matcher checks all registered patterns, invoking the associated method whenever a pattern is matched. For example, if a program editor announces when it has finished editing a module, a compiler might register for such announcements and automatically recompile the edited module.

To describe this behavior in terms of our basic model, we first define a new type of basic entity, *PATTERN*.

[*PATTERN*]

Next we associate a pattern matcher (*match*) with *EventSystem*, and a *register* relation that, for each component, associates patterns with methods of that component. The register relation then determines *EM*.

─── *Field* ───
EventSystem
match : *EVENT* ↔ *PATTERN*
register : *Component* ↔ (*PATTERN* × *METHOD*)
───────────────────────────────────
dom *register* ⊆ *components*
$((c_1.name, e), (c_2.name, m)) \in EM \Leftrightarrow$
$\quad\quad (\exists pat : PATTERN \bullet (c_2, (pat, m)) \in register \land (e, pat) \in match)$
──

The invariant guarantees that the Event/Method pairs in *EM* are those for which some registered pattern matches the event associated with the method.

What have we gained from this kind of formalization? First we have identified a common architectural abstraction (or style) shared by many systems. Second, we have exposed the similarities in two systems by showing how they are elaborations of the same basic formal architecture. Third, we have provided a template by which other kinds of comparisons can be made. (In other work, we have illustrated a number of these [GN91].) The formal model is simple enough that students in a senior/masters-level course on software architecture are able to provide their own specializations to show how blackboard systems and spreadsheets can be characterized in this way [GSO+92]. Third, although we have not indicated it here, it is possible to provide a complete semantics for such an architectural style by describing a computational model associated with it. For examples of such descriptions see [AG92, AAG93].

5   Steps Towards a Theory of Software Architecture

An important goal for researchers in software architecture is to clarify the basic nature of software architecture. What is a component? What is a connector? What might one mean by a "well-formed" architecture? What are reasonable rules for architectural decomposition, whereby a component or connector is itself represented by a sub-architecture?

A first step towards answering these questions is to develop a formal basis for describing and reasoning about architectural interaction. More specifically, we would like to have a formal foundation for architectural connectors. Ideally this would allow us to precisely characterize many basic kinds of connectors: procedure call, event broadcast, pipes, etc. Additionally, it would allow us to describe connectors that represent more complex interactions, such as those defined by network protocols, database query protocols, and client-server protocols. Finally, it would give us a way to check that an architectural description is well-formed, in the sense that components interact in ways consistent with the connector's specification.

We have developed a notation and supporting formalism, called WRIGHT, that does just that [AG94b]. The basic point of view is to treat an architecture as a graph of components and connectors. Components define the principal computations of a system, and connectors describe the interactions between components. In this model connectors are treated as first class objects that can be formally specified, decomposed, refined, and analyzed.

Figure 2 shows how a simple client-server system would be described in the WRIGHT architectural description language. The architecture of a system is described in three parts. The first part of the description defines the *component* and *connector* types. A component type is described as a set of *ports* and a *component-spec*. Each port defines a logical point of interaction between the component and its environment.[1] In this simple example Server and Client components both have a single port, but in general a component might might have more.

---

[1] Ports are *logical* entities: there is no implication that a port must be realized as a port of a task in an operating system.

```
System SimpleExample
    Component Server
        Port provide
            [provide protocol]
        Spec [Server specification]
    Component Client
        Port request
            [request protocol]
        Spec [Client specification]
    Connector C-S-connector
        Role client
            [client protocol]
        Role server
            [server protocol]
        Glue [glue protocol]
Instances
    s: Server
    c: Client
    cs: C-S-connector
Attachments
    s.provide as cs.server;
    c.request as cs.client
end SimpleExample.
```

Fig. 2. A Simple Client-Server System

A connector type is defined by a set of *roles* and a *glue* specification. The roles describe the expected behavior of each of the interacting parties. For example, the client-server connector illustrated above has a client role and a server role. The server role might describe the server's behavior as the alternate handling of requests and return of results. The glue specification describes how the activities of the client and server roles are coordinated. It would say that the activities must be sequenced in the order: client requests service, server handles request, server provides result, client gets result.

The second part of the overall system definition is a set of component and connector *instances*. These define the actual entities that will appear in the configuration. In the example, there is a single server (s), a single client (c), and a single C-S-connector instance (cs).

In the third part of the system definition, component and connector instances are combined by prescribing which component port are *attached as* (or instantiate) which connector roles. In the example the client request and server provide ports are attached as the client and server roles respectively. This means that the connector cs specifies the interactions between the ports c.request and s.provide. In a larger system, of course, there might be other instances of C-S-connector that define interactions between other ports.

The most novel aspect of a Wright specification is the use of protocols for defining connectors and the ports of components. The notation used for this is a variant of CSP [Hoa85]. To illustrate, a simplified form of a client-server connector might be written as follows:

connector C-S-connector =
    role Client = request!x→ result?y → Client ⊓ √
    role Server = invoke?x→ return!y → Server [] √
    glue = Client.request?x→ Service.invoke!x→Service.return?y
          →Client.result!y→**glue** [] √

The Client role describes the communication behavior of the user of the service. It is a protocol that can repeatedly request a service and then receive the result, or else terminate (indicated by √). The Server role describes the communication behavior of the Server. As with the Client role, it is defined as a protocol that repeatedly accepts a service request and then return a reply; or it can terminate with success. The **glue** process coordinates the behavior of the two roles by indicating how the events of the roles work together. In this case it indicates that the client and server events are interleaved in the expected fashion.

The expressiveness of the notation depends heavily on the ability to distinguish sources of choice in a protocol. In the case of the Client role, the decision to terminate is left to the client itself (by virtue of the CSP non-deterministic ⊓ operator). In the case of the Server role, however, the choice of termination is determined by the environment in which that protocol operates — i.e., by the **glue** and the Client roles — as indicated by the CSP [] operator. The **glue** allows the Client role to decide whether to call or terminate and then sequences the remaining three events and their data. Thus, the two choice operators permit us to distinguish formally between situations in which a given role is *obliged* to provide some services — the case of Server — and the situation in which a participant may take advantage of some services if it chooses to do so — the case of Client.

As a more complex example, Figure 3 illustrates how a pipe connector would be specified using WRIGHT.

Specification of interaction in WRIGHT has a number of important properities. First, it isolates the respective obligations of the participants in an interaction. Roles are distinguished from the coordinating glue in a way that partitions the overall problem of specification. Second, it provides a basis for checking compatibility of architectural descriptions. By matching the protocols of the "ports" of a component with those of the connector role to which it is attached it can be determined if the expectations of the connector are fulfilled by the attached component (and vice versa). Roughly speaking, this amounts to determining whether one finite state machine subsumes another. Third, it permits verification that a connector is internally consistent in the sense that the connector cannot deadlock in a non-successful state. Indeed, the notation is such that the checking for compatibility and internal consistency can be done automatically using model checking techniques. (See [AG94b] for details.)

What is the value of this kind of formalism? First, it allows us to provide precise characterizations of the interactions that can take place between components in a software architecture. Second, since it is based on an established formal base (of

```
connector Pipe =
    role Writer = write→Writer ⊓ close→ √
    role Reader =
        let ExitOnly = close→ √
        in let DoRead = (read→Reader [] read-eof→ExitOnly)
        in DoRead ⊓ ExitOnly
    glue = let ReadOnly = Reader.read→ReadOnly
                        [] Reader.read-eof→Reader.close→ √
                        [] Reader.close→ √
            in let WriteOnly = Writer.write→WriteOnly [] Writer.close→ √
            in Writer.write→glue
                [] Reader.read→glue
                [] Writer.close→ReadOnly
                [] Reader.close→WriteOnly
```

Fig. 3. A Pipe Connector

process algebras), there is a rich body of theory that can be applied. Third, it allows us to perform architecture-specific analysis, such as checking for compatibility and connector consistency.

6   Conclusions

As we have illustrated, different kinds of architectural formalism provide different benefits. A formal description of a specific system can precisely document a particular design and allow one to reason about the behavior of that system. A formal description of an architectural style allows one to characterize common architectural abstractions and idioms as well as to compare different uses of that idiom. A formal theory for software architecture can make clear the nature of architectural composition and provides analytical and mechanical leverage for characterizing and analyzing architectures.

This suggests that the enterprise of developing formal underpinnings for software architecture will continue to be a multi-faceted enterprise. We have briefly outlined three of those facets and expect to others in the future.

Acknowledgements

As a synthesis and survey of previous results, much of the material for this paper has been drawn from previously published papers coauthored with number of colleagues. The formalization of instrumentation systems represents joint work with Norm Delisle and others from Tektronix [DG90, GD90]. The formalization of implicit invocation systems represents collaborative work with David Notkin [GN91].

The formal basis for connectors is joint work with Robert Allen and parts of that section are adapted from [AG94b]. I gratefully acknowledge the contributions of these colleagues. In addition, I would like to thank Mary Shaw, Daniel Jackson, and Jeannette Wing for their help in clarifying the benefits and limitations of formal approaches to software architecture.

This research was sponsored by the National Science Foundation under Grant Number CCR-9357792, by the Wright Laboratory, Aeronautical Systems Center, Air Force Materiel Command, USAF, and the Advanced Research Projects Agency (ARPA) under grant number F33615-93-1-1330, and by Siemens Corporate Research. The views and conclusions contained in this document are those of the authors and should not be interpreted as representing the official policies, either expressed or implied, of Wright Laboratory, the U.S. Government, or Siemens Corporation.

References

[AAG93]   Gregory Abowd, Robert Allen, and David Garlan. Using style to give meaning to software architecture. In *Procedings of SIGSOFT'93: Foundations of Software Engineering*, December 1993.

[AG92]   Robert Allen and David Garlan. A formal approach to software architectures. In Jan van Leeuwen, editor, *Proceedings of IFIP'92*. Elsevier Science Publishers B.V., September 1992.

[AG94a]   Robert Allen and David Garlan. Beyond definition/use: Architectural interconnection. In *Proceedings of the ACM Interface Definition Language Workshop*, Portland, OR, January 1994. SIGPLAN Notices.

[AG94b]   Robert Allen and David Garlan. Formalizing architectural connection. In *Proceedings of the Sixteenth International Conference on Software Engineering*, May 1994.

[Ber92]   Alex Berson. *Client/Server Architecture*. McGraw Hill, 1992.

[DG90]   Norman Delisle and David Garlan. Applying formal specification to industrial problems: A specification of an oscilloscope. *IEEE Software*, September 1990.

[GD90]   David Garlan and Norman Delisle. Formal specifications as reusable frameworks. In *VDM'90: VDM and Z - Formal Methods in Software Development*, pages 150–163, Kiel, Germany, April 1990. Springer-Verlag, LNCS 428.

[GN91]   David Garlan and David Notkin. Formalizing design spaces: Implicit invocation mechanisms. In *VDM'91: Formal Software Development Methods*, pages 31–44, Noordwijkerhout, The Netherlands, October 1991. Springer-Verlag, LNCS 551.

[GSO+92] David Garlan, Mary Shaw, Chris Okasaki, Curtis Scott, and Roy Swonger. Experience with a course on architectures for software systems. In *Proceedings of the Sixth SEI Conference on Software Engineering Education*. Springer Verlag, LNCS 376, October 1992. Also available as a CMU/SEI technical report, CMU/SEI-92-TR-17.

[Hoa85]   C.A.R. Hoare. *Communicating Sequential Processes*. Prentice Hall, 1985.

[KP88]   G.E. Krasner and S.T. Pope. A cookbook for using the model-view-controller user interface paradigm in Smalltalk-80. *Journal of Object Oriented Programming*, 1(3):26–49, August/September 1988.

[NGGS93] David Notkin, David Garlan, William G. Griswold, and Kevin Sullivan. Adding implicit invocation to languages: Three approaches. In S. Nishio and A. Yonezawa, editors, *Proceedings of the JSSST International Symposium on Object Technologies for Advanced Software*, pages 489–510. Springer-Verlag LNCS, no. 742, November 1993.

[Rei90] Steven P. Reiss. Connecting tools using message passing in the field program development environment. *IEEE Software*, July 1990.

[SG93] Mary Shaw and David Garlan. Characteristics of higher-level languages for software architecture, 1993.

[Sha93] Mary Shaw. Procedure calls are the assembly language of system interconnection: Connectors deserve first-class status. In *Proceedings of the Workshop on Studies of Software Design*, May 1993.

[Spi89] J.M. Spivey. *The Z Notation: A Reference Manual.* Prentice Hall, 1989.

Difficulties with Object-Oriented Frameworks*

Gail C. Murphy and David Notkin

Department of Computer Science & Engineering, FR-35
University of Washington
Seattle, WA 98195 USA
{gmurphy,notkin}@cs.washington.edu

Abstract. The goal of an object-oriented framework is to provide a reusable design that supports the development of multiple related applications. In practice, frameworks are distributed as source code with little or no design documentation. This complicates both the instantiation and extension of these frameworks.

We illustrate this problem by examining the HotDraw framework, which provides 2D graphical editing capabilities in the Smalltalk environment. We used both the Smalltalk development environment tools and an existing framework design notation, Helm's contracts, to try to understand the framework. Our analysis of HotDraw using these approaches suggests that frameworks would be easier to instantiate and extend if more design and documentation effort were focused on two important framework interfaces: the interface exported to applications, and the interface exported to other frameworks. Based on this observation, we describe a set of usage dependences that are intended to improve framework interface design with respect to instantiation and extension.

1 Introduction

The goal of an object-oriented framework is to provide a reusable design that supports the development of multiple related applications. While most examples of object-oriented frameworks are in the domain of user interfaces (e.g., Model-View-Controller or MVC [1], InterViews [6] and ET++ [10]), frameworks in other domains are also available. For example, the CHOICES framework [4] supports the development of operating systems. Regardless of the domain, most frameworks do not capture and convey sufficient design information, complicating both the instantiation and extension of the frameworks.

We illustrate this problem by examining HotDraw [5], which we chose as a representative example of the current state of the art in object-oriented frameworks. HotDraw is a framework that provides 2D graphical editing capabilities

---

* This research was supported in part by the National Science Foundation under Grant Numbers CCR-9113367 and CCR-8858804 and by SRA (Tokyo Japan). The views and conclusions contained in this document are those of the authors and should not be interpreted as representing the official policies, either expressed or implied, of the U.S. Government, or of SRA.

in the Smalltalk environment. HotDraw is itself built from the Smalltalk MVC framework. To better understand HotDraw's design, we used both the tools available in the Smalltalk development environment and also the contracts notation [3] to analyze the behavioural interactions among the framework's classes.

Our analysis of HotDraw suggests that frameworks would be easier to instantiate and extend if more design effort was focused on two important framework interfaces: the interface exported to applications, and the interface exported to other frameworks. The ease of instantiating a framework is dependent upon the first interface, while the extensibility of a framework is dependent upon the latter interface. In addition, documentation for a framework must explicitly describe each of these interfaces. Using HotDraw as an example, we introduce the kinds of dependences important to consider in application-to-framework and framework-to-framework interfaces.

This paper is organized as follows. Section 2 provides background on object-oriented frameworks and describes how frameworks are commonly used today to support application development. Section 3 describes techniques for analyzing the design of frameworks using HotDraw as an example. Section 4 discusses the kinds of usage dependences in framework interfaces that must be considered during framework design. Section 5 concludes with a discussion of further research required to investigate and improve framework design.

2   Object-Oriented Frameworks

An object-oriented framework consists of "a collection of abstract and concrete classes and the interfaces between them" [11]. Three interfaces are of interest in an object-oriented framework [1]. First, there is the external interface provided to clients that instantiate the framework. Second, there is the internal interface provided to clients that subclass from the framework. Third, there is the resulting interface that is the combination of the external and internal interfaces.

Object-oriented frameworks are distinct from class libraries and applications. An object-oriented framework is distinct from a class library because the resulting interface of the framework may include unresolved behavioural interactions between classes of the framework. A framework is distinct from an application because an application is not required to export any interfaces.

When an application is built from a framework, inheritance is used to tailor and augment the behaviour of the framework. That is, the application developer specifies subclasses that implement the operations left unimplemented by the framework. Optionally, the developer may specify subclasses to override functionality from the framework or may define new classes that use the services of the framework. The application developer is also responsible for ensuring that the appropriate objects required by the framework are instantiated at execution.

An object-oriented framework may also be used to build another object-oriented framework. Similar to an application, a framework is built from another framework using inheritance and instantiation. However, whereas an application must ensure all unspecified framework behaviour is resolved, there are no such restrictions when a framework is the target.

Whether used to build another framework or to build an application, an object-oriented framework is not generally designed from scratch, but rather evolves from the development of several similar applications or frameworks.

Object-oriented frameworks are typically distributed as source code with little or no associated design information. Documentation for a framework is often organized according to classes of the framework and consists of natural language descriptions of the methods of a class. This is the approach taken in the documentation for the InterViews framework. This form of documentation makes it difficult for users of the framework to understand the exported interfaces. As a result, developers learn, use and extend the framework to build new applications by modifying example applications provided by the framework creators.

Documentation for the HotDraw framework takes a different approach using patterns [5] to describe the purpose of the framework. A pattern describes a problem that occurs in the domain addressed by the framework and explains how the framework may be used to solve the problem. For example, one of the HotDraw patterns describes how figures in a drawing may be grouped and treated as a single complex figure. Patterns are primarily oriented towards an application writer. There is insufficient experience with patterns to determine if they are an adequate mechanism to document the design of the framework-to-framework interface.

3 Using Frameworks

Without access to the framework design, developers build new applications from the framework by modifying existing examples. If the example is functionally similar to the target application, this is often sufficient. As the application begins to diverge from the example, the lack of understanding of the framework design makes it difficult to understand how to appropriately instantiate classes and create subclasses. In fact, it may even be difficult to judge whether or not the application is a suitable candidate for development from the framework.

Understanding the design of a framework requires knowledge of the structural and behavioural relationships that exist between its classes and between its objects. This requires an understanding of:

- the framework's class hierarchy,
- the semantic specification of each class in the framework,
- the abstract classes that require subclassing, and
- the required behavioural interactions between objects of the framework classes at execution.

3.1 Development Environment

The tools available to aid the developer in extracting this information from the framework source code vary with the language and environment in which the framework is implemented. A developer may gain some understanding of the class hierarchy, abstract classes, and semantics of classes in the framework through the use of browsers.

We used the Smalltalk browsers available in the Objectworks\Smalltalk product from ParcPlace Systems to gain an understanding of the static relationships between the HotDraw classes. By applying these tools to the HotDraw source code, we derived the view of the framework design illustrated in Fig. 1. The solid lines in Fig. 1 indicate the inheritance relationship between classes of HotDraw and the MVC framework.

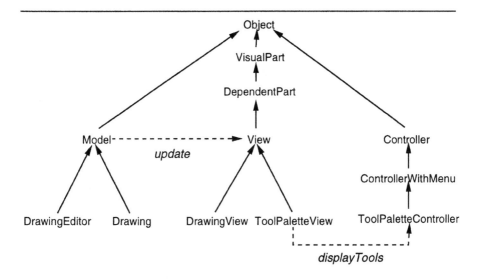

Fig. 1. HotDraw framework design using Smalltalk tools

It is more difficult for a developer to gain an understanding of the behavioural interactions between objects of the framework classes. We used the Smalltalk inspector to provide initial insight into the behavioural relationships between the HotDraw objects. The dashed lines in Fig. 1 indicate messages between objects of the framework classes. These messages do not provide full information about the required behavioural interactions. For example, it is implicit that as a result of a changed message to an instance of DrawingEditor, a subclass of Model, an update message is sent to ToolPaletteView, which in turn sends a displayTools message to the instance of ToolPaletteController to redisplay the DrawingEditor. Determining this interaction requires a detailed study of the source code of multiple classes and frameworks.

In a dynamically typed language like Smalltalk, an examination of the source code involves a reverse engineering of the types of instance variables and method arguments. This is necessary to understand the behavioural dependences between classes. For example, the Tool class in the HotDraw framework provides an abstract description of applying a Tool, like a paintbrush, to a drawing. The Tool class includes a Controller instance variable which is used to change a drawing. Determining the class of the Controller, if comments are not maintained, requires a study of the message protocol expected by the Controller. There are no tools in the Smalltalk language environment to automatically extract the required information.

3.2 Contracts

One technique that appears to help make explicit the behavioural interactions unsupported by the language environment tools is the contract specification approach [3]. Contracts specify behavioural dependences between objects, preconditions for establishing contracts, and invariants to be maintained by objects participating in contracts.

Figure 2 shows fragments of two contracts we wrote to describe the HotDraw framework. The first contract fragment describes the MVC framework. In particular, this contract describes the behavioural dependences required to maintain consistency between a model and its set of views and controllers. A Model within an MVC triad has a registered set of View objects. When a Model is altered, it sends itself the changed message which causes an update message to be sent to each registered View. The MVC contract fragment includes an unresolved behavioural dependency between a View and its Model (the update method on a View). This is indicated by the lack of a formal specification of the behaviour of a View when it receives an update message. The second contract fragment, the HotDraw contract, describes how the visual appearance of tools available in the editor is maintained. This HotDraw contract refines the MVC contract by specifying the dependency between the ToolPaletteView and its associated Controller on an update operation, a dependency left unspecified by the MVC contract.

The use of contracts to analyze the HotDraw framework provided insight into the design of the framework. For example, the contracts provided a view of how the interactions of an object are grouped by the contracts in which it participates, identifying the contexts in which one object depends upon another. This view helps to clarify where and how a developer may extend the design of the framework to build an application. For example, based on the contracts shown in Fig. 2, a developer can determine that the ToolPaletteView relies on an associated Controller to redraw the visual appearance of the tools when the DrawingEditor changes. This provides context for the Controller's dependence on the DrawingEditor.

While contracts were a useful formalism for analyzing the behavioural aspects of the framework, they do not clearly illustrate the structural relationships between objects. For example, to determine the structural relationship between Models and Views, one must study the bundling of the Model and View specifications in one contract, as well as the specification of the behaviour required to

contract MVC

> *This contract describes the behavioural relationships between the Model,*
> *View and Controller objects. Each Model object may have one or more*
> *Views visible.*

Model **supports**
    addDependent(aView) $\rightarrow$ { Views$'$ = Views $\cup$ {aView} }
    changed(aSymbol) $\rightarrow$ $\langle$ $\|$ v, v $\in$ Views: v.update (aSymbol) $\rangle$

Views: Set(View) **where each** View **supports**
    setModel(aModel) $\rightarrow$ { Model = aModel }
    update(aSymbol) $\rightarrow$ { View reflects Model }

  etc.
end contract

contract HotDraw

> *This contract describes the behavioural relationships between the essential*
> *HotDraw classes. HotDraw builds on the MVC framework.*

refines
    MVC (Model = DrawingEditor
           Views = { ToolPaletteView, DrawingView })
        etc.

DrawingEditor **supports**
    – no refined behaviour from Model, no new behaviour

ToolPaletteView **supports**
    update(aSymbol) $\rightarrow$ { Controller.displayTools }

DrawingView **supports**
    update(aSymbol) $\rightarrow$ { }

  etc.
end contract

Fig. 2. Contracts describing the HotDraw framework

keep the relationship consistent (i.e., the addDependent behaviour on a Model). Not only is the one-to-many cardinality of the relationship between Models and Views implicit, but there is no indicator to identify which behaviour specifications in the contract are providing support for maintaining consistency between objects in the specification and which are providing behaviour directly related to the functionality supported by the objects.

4 Discussion

Our analysis of the HotDraw framework raises several questions about how, in general, to design, document and use object-oriented frameworks. In particular, the analysis drew attention to two important aspects of framework design that are all too often left implicit: the interface offered by the framework to applications, and the interface offered to other frameworks.

4.1 Application-to-Framework Interface

Building a new, functionally appropriate application from the HotDraw framework is not particularly difficult, normally requiring the subclassing and instantiation of only the DrawingEditor class. The DrawingEditor class in HotDraw exports an interface to the application that includes a defaultTools message. The defaultTools message may be overridden in a subclass to change the tools offered by the editor. This is the mechanism used by HotPaint — a sample application distributed with HotDraw — to offer a specialized 2D drawing editor built on the HotDraw framework.

In most frameworks, however, more classes and objects must be appropriately defined by an application. Ensuring that the required structural and behavioural interactions between these classes and objects are met is difficult in the absence of proper design information. For example, building an application from the MVC framework requires, at a minimum, subclassing the Model and View classes to ensure that the update method on View is able to query the Model for its current state (see the contract fragment in Fig. 2), the instantiation of Model, View and Controller objects, and the registration of the View object with the Model object.

The design information must convey to the application writer the instantiation and subclassing necessary for the framework to be used privately by the application. A private use of a framework does not require the application to re-export the interface provided either to other frameworks, or to the application. The design information for any necessary subclassing, however, must convey whether inherited behaviour may be redefined completely or may only be augmented. Current design notations and tools are insufficient for conveying this information to the application writer.

4.2 Framework-to-Framework Interface

Extending the HotDraw framework is complicated both because of the lack of explicit design information and also because of inappropriate dependences among classes and objects in the framework. For example, extending the framework to handle multiple views for a Drawing — an extension that seems especially natural in the MVC paradigm — is difficult because of the way in which HotDraw builds on the MVC framework. In particular, HotDraw's DrawingView class is registered as a dependent View of the DrawingEditor class, a subclass of the MVC Model class, but the semantic contents of the DrawingView are managed by the Drawing class. This makes extension harder because the semantic information for the DrawingView class is not stored in its Model, the DrawingEditor. To help alleviate problems like these, we have identified three different ways in which frameworks exploit other frameworks.

First, one framework may generalize the original framework by augmenting the services available between classes. This is illustrated in Fig. 3 where the MVC framework is generalized to support the ability to reflect changes in views back to models. The dashed arrows between classes in Fig. 3 represent message dependences between the classes. Message categories, like update messages, are indicated in italics. The solid lines in Fig. 3 indicate inheritance relationships. Although the derivation of the bi-directional MVC framework from the original MVC framework would be considered a refinement in the traditional object-oriented sense, from the point of view of the behavioural abstraction captured by the framework, it is a generalization. The generalized bi-directional MVC framework exports the same interface as the MVC framework and more. This generalization information must be conveyed to the designer of the exploiting framework.

Second, one framework may refine another framework. This is also illustrated in Fig. 3 where the bi-directional MVC framework is refined to support the behavioural abstraction between a Drawing, a DrawingView and a Drawing-Controller in HotDraw. The refined framework exports the same interface as the bi-directional MVC framework but also adds more specialized behaviour. Both the generalization and specialization framework dependences, then, preserve the original framework interface.

Third, one framework may privately use another framework. Figure 3 depicts a private use of a framework in terms of framework aggregation where the DrawingEditor class of the HotDraw framework aggregates two refinements of the MVC framework – the Drawing MVC triad and a ToolPalette MVC triad. This corresponds to the private use of a framework (HotDraw) by an application (HotPaint). The application and framework interface exported by the original framework is not re-exported by the new framework.

The framework dependences described above do not necessarily translate directly to an object-oriented inheritance structure. For instance, the generalization dependence described above may be implemented by re-creating the MVC framework as a specialization of the bi-directional framework. However, the information captured by the dependence about the interface the framework exports is crucial for designers of frameworks and applications who use the generalized framework to evolve their own software.

These usage dependences suggest an evolutionary path to increase the extensibility of HotDraw. The generalization dependence described in Fig. 3 does not require any changes to the current implementation as the functionality is already present in the Smalltalk MVC classes. The dependence, though, indicates the intent of the designer to exploit the additional behaviour. The refinement dependence between the MVC framework and the ToolPalette MVC framework requires the introduction of a new class, the ToolPalette class. The introduc-

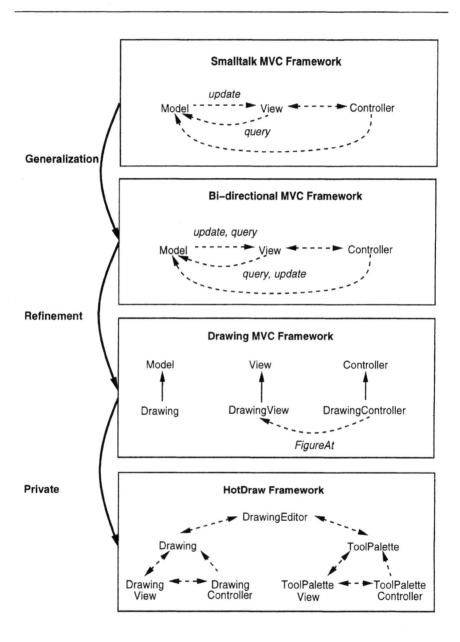

Fig. 3. Framework-to-Framework usage dependences

tion of the ToolPalette MVC framework also changes the instantiation of the HotDraw framework as two refinements of the MVC framework, the Drawing MVC and the ToolPalette MVC frameworks, must now be instantiated. The private dependence permits changes to the application interface exported by the HotDraw framework. For example, the HotDraw framework may export the Drawing and ToolPalette MVC framework interfaces to permit tailoring of the kind of DrawingViews or ToolPaletteViews used with the framework. This restructuring would permit the definition of multiple views of a Drawing consistent with the design of the framework.

Object-oriented frameworks in common use today generally consist of tens to hundreds of classes. The importance of the interface exported by the framework to both applications and other frameworks suggests that object-oriented frameworks may be more extensible if they were constructed as aggregations and refinements of smaller frameworks. When extending frameworks built in this manner, usage dependences could be chosen to have the desired effect on the exported interfaces. Design notations could be used to describe the semantics of the framework with usage dependences describing the interactions between frameworks.

5 Summary

Frameworks are a good idea. They have been used to increase reuse. However, to increase their benefit requires several improvements.

First, documenting the design of a framework is essential. Notations for capturing both the structural and behavioural relationships within a framework's design and also the interfaces exported by the framework are needed. A notation for specifying the interfaces exported by a framework must be capable of expressing unresolved behavioural dependences and the constraints on those dependences. Current notations, such as contracts and others used throughout the object-oriented design world (e.g., collaboration graphs [12] and OMT [9]), are insufficient to capture this design information. In addition, tools are needed to help derive the design of existing frameworks. Browsers and inspectors provide only partial information about a framework's design.

Second, properly documenting a framework's design does not necessarily make it easy to instantiate or extend. Reducing dependences among classes and objects in the framework requires careful design of application and framework interfaces. To improve existing frameworks in this dimension requires that they be restructured.

We are planning several activities to investigate improvements along these lines. First, we are investigating how static typing policies for common object-oriented languages may help to maintain structural and behavioural constraints when instantiation, refinement and generalization operations are applied to frameworks [7]. Second, Opdyke has identified a set of restructuring primitives, called refactorings, for object-oriented systems and frameworks [8]. Refactorings are behaviour preserving and use class invariants and component member variables to determine the design intent. We plan to try to restructure the HotDraw framework using Opdyke's refactorings. This will give us insight into both the power of these refactorings and the role the three framework usage dependences may have in restructuring. Third, we plan to explore automated support for restructuring of frameworks, based on Griswold's approach [2] in which a tool guarantees equivalence between the original and the restructured system. Finally, we plan to consider appropriate tools and notations for documenting framework designs.

References

[1] DEUTSCH, L. P. *Design Reuse and Frameworks in the Smalltalk-80 System*. ACM Press, 1989, ch. A.3.

[2] GRISWOLD, W. G., AND NOTKIN, D. Automated Assistance for Program Restructuring. *ACM Transactions on Software Engineering and Methodology 2*, 3 (July 1993), 228-269.

[3] HELM, R., HOLLAND, I. M., AND GANGOPADHYAY, D. Contracts: Specifying Behavioral Compositions in Object-Oriented Systems. In *Proc. of the OOPSLA '89 Conf. on Object-oriented Programming Systems, Languages and Applications* (1990), 169–180.

[4] JOHNSON, R. AND RUSSO, V. Reusing Object-Oriented Designs. Department of Computer Science, Tech. Rep. UIUCDCS 91-1696, University of Illinois, 1991.

[5] JOHNSON, R. Documenting Frameworks using Patterns. In *Proc. of the OOPSLA '92 Conf. on Object-oriented Programming Systems, Languages and Applications* (1992), 63–76.

[6] LINTON, M. A., VLISSIDES, J. M., AND CALDER, P. R. Composing User Interfaces with InterViews. *IEEE Computer 22*, 2 (February 1989), 8–22.

[7] MURPHY, G. C. AND NOTKIN, D. The Interaction Between Static Typing and Frameworks. Department of Computer Science and Engineering, Tech. Rep. 93-09-02, University of Washington, 1993.

[8] OPDYKE, W. *Refactoring Object-Oriented Frameworks*. PhD thesis, University of Illinois at Urbana-Champaign, 1992.

[9] RUMBAUGH, J., BLAHA, M., PREMERLANI, W., EDDY, F., AND LORENSEN, W. *Object-Oriented Modeling and Design*. Prentice-Hall, 1991.

[10] WEINAND, A., GAMMA, E., AND MARTY, R. Design and Implementation of ET++, A Seamless Object-Oriented Application Framework. In *Proc. of the OOPSLA '88 Conf. on Object-oriented Programming Systems, Languages and Applications* (1988), 46–57.

[11] WIRFS-BROCK, R., AND JOHNSON, R. Surveying Current Research in Object-Oriented Design. *Communications of the ACM 33*, 9 (September 1990), 104–124.

[12] WIRFS-BROCK, R., WILKERSON, B., AND WIENER, L. *Designing Object-Oriented Software*. Prentice-Hall, 1990.

Using a Metasystem Approach to Support and Study the Design Process

Paul G. Sorenson
Department of Computing Science
University of Alberta
Edmonton, Alberta T6G 2H1
sorenson@cs.ualberta.ca

J.-Paul Tremblay
Department of Computational Science
University of Saskatchewan
Saskatoon, Saskatchewan S7N 0W0
deview@cs.usask.ca

Abstract

This paper describes ways in which the Metaview metasystem has been used to support and study various approaches to software design. The EARA/GE meta model is described and illustrated with the definition of a structure chart design environment. The use of Metaview in the support of transformations to design and expression of design metrics is demonstrated. Support for the capture of design rationale and automatic software diagram layout are discussed. Conclusions and future research directions are provided at the end of the paper.

1 Introduction

Providing adequate support environments for the development of software has been a recognized problem for many years. Several support environments have been developed to aid in the requirement analysis and design phases. Commercial CASE environments have been introduced that apply these concepts to the entire life cycle. These environments are meant to support the production of many diagrammatic techniques [14]. The effort to develop such environments is considerable, as are enhancements or changes to a support environment to address an application's special requirements. To reduce significantly the effort of producing a support environment, some researchers have proposed metasystems [9]. Research project prototypes adopting this approach include: Metaview[22], Socrates[25], MetaPlex[7] and MetaEdit[21]). The main goal of a metasystem is to generate automatically much of the software necessary for a specification environment. The benefits of using a metasystem include:

- a great reduction in the time and cost to develop a computer-aided environment is achieved;

- the formal description of a particular environment is less ambiguous and easier to understand and analyze (as to consistency and completeness) than an informal one;

- the underlying model which is inherent in the metasystem acts as a framework for improving and modifying an existing computer-aided specification environment; and

- a comparison of alternative environments, such as those for supporting the design process [10], is facilitated by contrasting definitions expressed in a common metasystem description.

This paper begins with a description of the metasystem architecture for *Metaview* and its associated data model (including graphical extension) used in specifying and producing specification environments. Such environments are concerned with the creation and manipulation of a variety of software specification objects. Section 3 concentrates primarily on ways our metasystem supports design activities. These include the specification of CASE (Computer-Assisted Software Engineering) tool support for some well-known design methodologies as well as the capture of design rationale when performing software design. Section 4 summarizes the paper and discusses future work.

2   The *Metaview* Approach to Generating Specification Environments

The main goal of a metasystem is to generate automatically a large part of the software necessary for CASE environments [9]. This is accomplished in Metaview through the EARA (Entity-Attribute-Relationship-Aggregate) model and its GE (graphical extension) which is used to define the software specification objects.

2.1   Metasystem Architecture

In Metaview, we have adopted a generative approach to the creation of software specification environments using a metasystem that is analogous to the use of compiler-compiler systems in the development compilers. There are three levels of specification in most metasystems: the *meta level*, the *environment level*, and the *user level*. The user in this case is the analyst/designer.

At the *meta level*, the Metaview definer defines the specification data model (or meta model) for the metasystem. This will be described in Section 2.2. The *meta definer* is also responsible for the creation of the database engine, the environment-model-processor (compiler), and the tool set facilities.

At the *environment level*, the *environment definer* specifies an environment definition. The environment definition includes an environment model definition, plus tool-specific information for that environment. The environment model definition is expressed as an Environment Description Language (EDL)/ Environment Constraint Language (ECL) program which is processed by the environment-model-processor (compiler). The compiler produces a set of tables describing the software objects and their inter-relationships, as well as a set of constraints that apply to these objects. The EDL compiler was generated by the ATS parser generator system [24].

Each tool in the environment is configured using the environment tables and any tool specific information for that environment.

At the *user level*, analysts/designers select a particular specification environment that has been configured. This environment includes a generalized environment model analyzer, a database engine, and a set of environment tools. Several different tools may interact with a specification at the user level. These tools include batch definition tools, graphically interactive tools, report generator tools, verification tools, etc. These facilities are used to store and analyze specifications for any software system the analysts/designers want to define. Each specification is stored in a specification database.

2.2   The EARA/GE Data Model

Before an environment definition language is created, the information required to support a general specification environment definition must be modeled. As well, special-purpose specification databases conforming to this definition must also be defined.

The EARA model [15] is based in part on the Entity Relationship (ER) model [8]. The meta model must also contain features that permit semantic-based data modeling. These features include the abstraction mechanism of aggregation, generalization, and classification. These features are needed to properly model the hierarchical nature of relationships among components in a complex system.

The meta model must support a specification schema that contains the following set of descriptive elements.

AgT:	A finite set of aggregate type names.
ET:	A finite set of entity type names.
RT:	A finite set of relationship type names.
AN:	A finite set of attribute names.
RN:	A finite set of role names.
VTD:	A finite set of value type definitions.

The sets *AgT, ET, RT, AN* and *RN* are distinct (i.e., their intersection is the empty set).

An EARA specification scheme also has a set of mapping functions [22] for attribute association, role mapping, relationship participation and generalization. A special set of functions deals with aggregation. These include the component type function, which specifies the types of entities and relationships that can be components of each type of aggregate. The *aggregate identification function* maps an aggregate type name to an entity type name. This allows an aggregate which is composed of many entities and relationships, to be treated as a single identifiable entity within another aggregate. In effect, subaggregates of a given entity can be identified as special types of entities called *aggregate entities.* The set of design objects in the aggregation is called an *aggregate component.* It should be stressed that aggregates are "first class citizens" in the data model. Aggregation is an indispensable feature in modeling various decomposition approaches used in design methodologies.

A graphical extension (GE) to the EARA model has been designed [20]. The extension supports the definition of a graphical representation for software objects definable in the basic EARA model. The representations are intended for the development of interactive and layout tools that allow analysts/designers to manipulate descriptions in a specification database using a graphical workstation.

More specifically, six component types are identified in the GE extension: *diagrams, icons, edges, labels, subdiagrams,* and *adornments.* The definition of the relationship between the EARA objects and the GE objects include the following types of functions:

- *Association functions:* These formally map a graphical object type to its corresponding specification object type.

- *Characterization functions:* These map a label to a particular diagram, icon, or edge type.

- *Diagram component function:* This function maps a set of icons, labels, or edges to a diagram, thus formalizing the diagram as an aggregate object type in the GE extension.

- *Diagram explosion function:* This function maps an aggregate icon to a diagram.

This completes our brief overview of the EARA/GE model. In the next section we describe how Metaview can support the software design process.

3 Metaview Support for the Design Process

This section briefly describes how Metaview has been used to support: the generation of specification environments for different design paradigms; the specification of design transformations to produce a design; the inclusion of software metrics for assessing the quality of the design process and the design product; the specification of a tool to capture design rationale; and the specification and generation of an automatic diagram layout facility for producing different design diagram types such as structure charts.

3.1 Modeling and Generating Tools for Design Methodologies

Several design methodologies have been modeled including Structured Design [18][26], Higher-Order Software (HOS) [13] and the ADISSA methodology [2][12]. This section focuses on the modeling of a structure chart environment to support Structured Design.

A structure chart shows the partitioning of a software system into a hierarchy of modules. The basic elements of a structure chart are given in Figure 1, which depicts the graphical representation of a standard module, a library module, the invocation of a module as represented by a directed edge, data couple, control couple, loop control, decision control, a data file, and an external interface. Examples of structure charts which exhibit the use of the basic symbols appear in Figure 2.

An EDL program description for a structure chart environment begins with the following declaration:

ENVIRONMENT_NAME structure_charts;

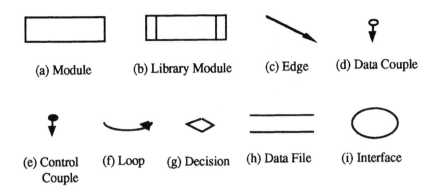

Figure 1. Basic graphic symbols for structure chart

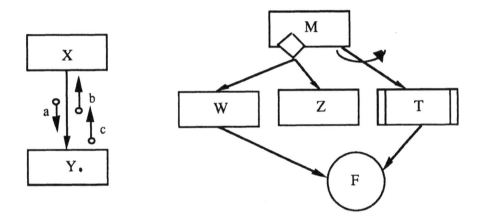

Figure 2. Examples of structure charts

Upper-case names denote keywords and lower-case names are created by the environment definer.

The following EDL statements defines the various classes of entities in the environment.

```
ENTITY_TYPE universal GENERIC
    ATTRIBUTES (description: text);
ENTITY_TYPE any_module GENERIC IS_A universal,
    module IS_A any_module,
    library_module IS_A any_module;
ENTITY_TYPE control_structure GENERIC IS_A universal,
    transaction_center IS_A control_structure,
```

```
            iteration IS_A control_structure;
    ENTITY_TYPE data_object GENERIC IS_A universal,
            data_couple IS_A data_object,
            control_couple IS_A data_object;
    ENTITY_TYPE module_specification IS_A universal;
    ENTITY_TYPE data_file IS_A universal
        ATTRIBUTES (form: string(1..30));
    ENTITY_TYPE interface IS_A universal;
```

The entity class **universal** denotes the root class of the taxonomy of entity classes. The keyword GENERIC denotes that a class has descendant classes; i.e., the class is a non-leaf node in the taxonomy tree.

The EDL description defining the various relationship types for the structure chart environment follows. The symbol "I" denotes the "alternation" ("or") operator.

```
    RELATIONSHIP_TYPE calls
        ROLES (calling_module, called_module)
        PARTICIPANTS (module | control_structure, any_module);

    RELATIONSHIP_TYPE contains
        ROLES (container, element)
        PARTICIPANTS (module, control_structure);

    RELATIONSHIP_TYPE passing_data_couple
        ROLES (sender, data_element, receiver)
        PARTICIPANTS (any_module, data_couple, any_module);

    RELATIONSHIP_TYPE passing_control_couple
        ROLES (sender, control_element, receiver)
        PARTICIPANTS (any_module, control_couple, any_module);

    RELATIONSHIP_TYPE file_access
        ROLES (name, data)
        PARTICIPANTS (any_module, data_file);

    RELATIONSHIP_TYPE accepts
        ROLES (name, user)
        PARTICIPANTS (module, interface);

    RELATIONSHIP_TYPE specifies_module
        ROLES (name, specification)
        PARTICIPANTS (any_module, module_specification);
```

A module can be decomposed or expanded into its constituent parts or components, as defined in the following EDL description of an aggregate:

```
    ENTITY_TYPE sc_agg
        BECOMES module_explosion;
```

```
AGGREGATE_TYPE module_explosion
COMPONENTS (ALL);
```

The first statement associates an entity type name, sc_agg with an aggregate type name, module_explosion. This permits an aggregate instance to be replaced by its associated base entity instance in a structure chart. The second statement states that a module_explosion can contain any entity type, relationship type and the aggregate type as components.

3.2 Transformation Approach to Supporting Software Design

If Metaview is to support software design successfully it must permit specifications defined during requirements definition to be transformed into design specifications. We recognized this quite early in the development of Metaview and augmented our EDL/ECL definition capability with ETL, the Environment Transformation Language [5]. ETL is a production rule oriented language in which each transformation description contains the following language characteristics:

- name of the transformation
- identification of the participating environments
- declared global data elements
- set of rules governing the transformation

Each rule has the following detail:

- name of the rule
- antecedent part, containing:
  - definition of EARA object types used in the rule
  - specification of conditions that hold before the execution of an action
- consequence part, containing:
  - mapping statements relating object types in the source environment definition to those in the target environment definition
  - actions to create instances of object types
  - oracle (i.e., analyst/designer) interventions

As an example, a rather straightforward rule create_modules follows. This rule assists in mapping process specifications in a data flow diagram environment to module specifications in an structure chart environment. In this example, it is assumed that a fully exploded data flow diagram is already partitioned into blocks (or subsets) of processes, each block associated with some characteristic such as whether the processes are all afferent, transform or efferent processes.

```
RULE create_modules;
*** Each subset of processes is mapped within its partition.
    INTEGER: i;
    process: p;
    process_specification: ps;
    module: m;
    module_specification: ms;
```

*** Modules are created and the mapping from process to module is
*** established.
*** Each process specification is migrated to the corresponding module
*** specification.

```
FOR i <- 1 TO ENDOF(s)
    FOR EACH p ε s[i]
        CREATE ENTITY module(m);
        mod[i] <- mod[i] U m;
        ORACLE OUTPUT 'Please provide module name for process: ';
        ORACLE OUTPUT p.name;
        ORACLE INPUT m.name;
        MAP p TO m;
        CREATE ENTITY module_specification(ms);
        CREATE RELATIONSHIP specifies_module(m,ms);
        MAP ps TO ms;
    ENDFOR;
ENDFOR;
```

In the example transformation rule, a module is created for each process in a block s[i]. The mapping function MAP is used to transform attributes associated with a source entity (e.g., a process p) to corresponding attributes in the target entity (e.g., a module m). The indexed set mod[i] is used to collect all modules created from a common block of processes s[i]. Interaction with the designer takes place through ORACLE INPUT and OUTPUT statements.

We have conducted two major studies involving the transformations of requirement specifications into design specifications. In the first study [5], we examined the transformation of a data flow diagram (DFD) requirements specification to a structure chart (SC) design specification based on the approach described in [18]. The main ETL rule set that describes the transformation contains five rules for analyzing the source environment, seven rules for constructing an initial structure chart based on a data flow diagram source specification, and three post transformation rules to analyze certain features and remove redundancies from the resulting design. Three important aspects that were discovered while modeling this transformation activity were:

- The need for oracle (i.e., analyst/designer) intervention was essential for this type of transformation (i.e, this transformation process could not be completely automated). In particular, expert assistance was needed in the initial partitioning of the DFD prior to transform or transaction analysis, in mapping processes to modules, and in creating the module hierarchy.

- The notion of a transformation attribute was required to assist in characterizing some of the specification objects as part of the transformation activities. Specifically, it was convenient to extend the definition of the process specification object to include an attribute called type which was assigned one of three possible values ('A' for afferent, 'E' for efferent, and 'T' for transform). These values correspond to the process type as identified in transform analysis [18]. Several other transformation attributes were used in the transformation rules for this study.

- The complexity of developing a rule set for what appeared to be a relatively simple, straightforward transformation was underestimated. A rather large set of complicated rules was necessary, many of which were required to cope with the informality of the structured analysis to structured design transformation approach. Transformation specification is a complex, tedious and error-prone task.

Based on the results of this study, several features of our first version of ETL were modified or enhanced and several new features were added to the language. The modified language was used in a second study [12] involving the ADISSA methodology [2]. This methodology prescribes the transformation of a requirements specification in the form of a DFD to a design specification in the form of a finite state machine (FSM) definition. The transformations in this approach were more complex than the Structured Analysis to Structured Design transformations. The steps involved a) determining basic transactions (called ADISSA transactions) in an extended form of DFD, b) converting ADISSA transactions to FSM transactions, and c) converting FSM transactions to FSM representations. Lessons learned from this second study include:

- Metrics, such as the total number of elementary processes and the total number of data elements moving into or out of an elementary process, could be embedded easily in the transformation rules to assist in the transformation process.

- Design stage metrics can be pre-computed at the analysis phase. For example, the metric STI (number of state transitions into a state) can be computed in advance of the transformation. Based on pre-design stage analysis of control data flow, it may be advisable to undertake a more detailed requirements analysis to determine if system simplifications can be achieved prior to the commencement of a detail design.

- Maintenance of transformation rules is difficult in the face of changes to the source or target environment definitions. A total of 24 rules were required to describe the transformation process. As we gained a greater understanding of the ADISSA transformation, it was necessary to change several aspects of the source and target environments. Changes to these environments caused several alterations to the transformations rules. We discovered that the problem of maintaining these rules in the face of environment changes was a non-trivial task.

- ADISSA is a formal transformation methodology that requires some designer input. Reverse transformations, which may be needed in re-engineering, require special support. In particular, the design decisions (or rationale) made during forward engineering must be recorded for later use to achieve reverse engineering using code abstraction concepts [6]. We concluded that more research into this problem must be undertaken.

3.3 The Specification of Software Metrics for Design Process Environments

A metasystem can be used to define suitable software metrics for a particular software specification environment. In this approach, metrics applicable to a particular specification environment (e.g., a structure chart environment) are defined in conjunction with the formal definition of that environment given in EDL. The metrics can be stated in Environment Transformation Language (ETL). The goal of this metrics approach is to incorporate, with relative ease, the metric computation into the software specification environment.

In [3], we proposed a metric-driven approach to software development with the principle characteristic of providing immediate feedback of system measurements to developers. The integration of the software process model definition and the software development environment definition, supplemented with measurement of products and processes, is a requirement for the successful development of large software systems. For example, in a structure chart environment suitable metrics could include module coupling, fan-in and fan-out. These could be used "on demand" by the designer to assist in evaluating the quality of the design based on certain coupling and cohesion principles.

To illustrate how metrics can be specified as part of the environment definition, consider the following metric *DAi* (as suggested by DeMarco), which for each module provides a count of the data tokens explicitly shared with that module:

```
RULE count_data_tokens;
    ENTITY ATTR INTEGER OF module: da
    any_module: m, n;
    data_object: p;
    FOR EACH m IN SET OF any_module
        m.da <- 0;
        FOR EACH n IN SET OF any_module WHERE calls(m,n)
            m.da <- COUNT p IN SET OF data_object
                    WHERE passing_control_couple(m,p,n) OR
                    passing_data_couple(m,p,n) OR
                    passing_control_couple(n,p,m) OR
                    passing_data_couple(n,p,m);
        ENDFOR;
        FOR EACH n IN SET OF any_module WHERE calls(n,m)
            m.da <- COUNT p IN SET OF data_object
                    WHERE passing_control_couple(m,p,n) OR
                    passing_data_couple(m,p,n) OR
                    passing_control_couple(n,p,m) OR
                    passing_data_couple(n,p,m);
        ENDFOR;
        *** The number of data tokens of the module is output.
        OUTPUT m.name, m.da
    ENDFOR;
```

In our research we have examined the representation of metrics for data flow diagrams, structure charts, resource flow graphs [17] and ADISSA finite state transactions [2]. The major conclusions from this study are:

- The incorporation of metric descriptions with environment definitions (for example, as part of ETL rules) is feasible.

- Most of the metrics encountered were expressible using simple count functions performed over specification objects. Further study is needed and more direct support should be considered for the computation of the level of a component within a hierarchy or the length of a relationship chain between specification objects.

- A triggering mechanism must be implemented to ensure that metrics can be evaluated immediately and yet be flexible enough to let designers choose to have the metrics computed after the entire design or parts of the design are completed. We are currently assessing and plan on adapting mechanisms suggested in the area of active databases [16].

- We have largely ignored the area of process metrics. This should be examined in conjunction with investigations of process environments [4].

3.4   Support for Design Rationale

We have used Metaview to model a Design Rationale System. Design rationale, in its simplest sense, examines the decisions made during the design process and the reasons as to why they were made. Capturing design rationale consists of recording the design decisions and the reasoning behind the design, which can be later analyzed to control the overall design and manage the complexity of the design process. The availability of design rationale will also have a major impact on maintenance effort and software evolution more generally. A survey of design rationale from a software engineering perspective is found in [11].

Capturing design rationale requires a data model for encapsulating design decisions and analysis information as the design evolves. A data model of a design process artifact is depicted in Figure 3. This ER-based model is an extension of a generic model proposed by [19]. It has six types of entities: artifact, step, position, issue, argument and header. An *artifact* represents information about a design state. A *step* is basically a design step used in producing refinements and revisions and is defined as an operation which creates or modifies artifacts. *Issues, positions,* and *arguments* make explicit the reasoning behind design decisions. A *header* is an entity which is linked to a step or issue by a special binary relation *updates*. The relation is binary as at any instant of time either step or issues updates the header. Step updates header when it modifies an artifact, i.e., is a clarification or deliberation to an already existing issue. An artifact has an attribute *status* which can have a value of active or processed, depending upon whether the artifact has been fully resolved (processed) or is still evolving (active). An *issue* also has an attribute *status*, which can have values of pending, processed, or ignored. A header plays a very important role in capturing design rationale. It contains all the information regarding who, what, when, and why a particular action was taken on a design artifact. More details on the header can be found in [1]. This data model has been defined using the EARA model. From this definition Metaview can be used to generate a design rationale support tool.

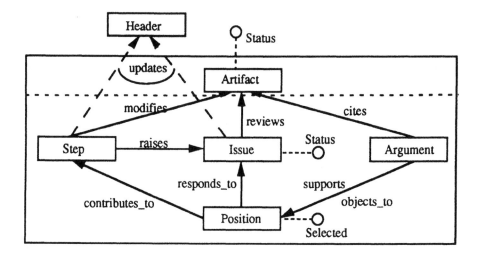

Figure 3. Design process artifact

3.5 Automatic Diagram Layout Support Facility

A useful tool in performing the design process is an automatic layout system for producing various types of design diagrams such as structure charts and HOS diagrams. We have surveyed automated layout systems and proposed an architecture for an automated diagram layout generation system [20] for various diagrammatic types. A central part of this system is a placement algebra for specifying constraints for icon placement, arc routing, and, more generally, diagram orientations and constraints.

The placement algebra consists of several operations on pairs of graphical objects such as *above, below, left_of, right_of, in_vertical_line, in_horizontal_line, next_to, centered_above, centered_below,* and *contained_within.* The placement algebra also deals with a graphical object's relationship to the diagram as well as to other graphical objects using the operations *contained_within, on_exterior_of, center_of, top_center_of,* and *on_border_of.* Some special properties of graphical objects such as *replicated_in* and *unique_in* are defined.

It is possible to categorize diagrams according to their orientation, that is, whether the diagram is read from top to bottom, left to right, etc. Software diagrams can be broken down into three basic orientations: *top-down, left-right,* and *not fixed.* An example of a diagram with top-down orientation is a structure chart; an example of a diagram with left-right orientation is a left-to-right decision tree; and some entity relationship diagrams have no fixed orientation.

The orientation of a diagram can determine how certain basic relationships are expressed graphically. For example, in hierarchical diagrams like structure charts and decision trees, one node can be considered the parent of one or more nodes. In a top-down diagram like a structure chart, a parent will always be above its children, who themselves will be placed in a horizontal line, while in a left-right diagram a parent will be to the left of its children, who will appear in a vertical line. Thus, once the orientation of a diagram is known and understood, it is possible to systematically define placements of icons according to that orientation.

4 Conclusions and Future Directions

We have described the Metaview metasystem, its underlying data model, and some of its uses in supporting the design process.

The study of transformations between stages (phases) of software development and the modeling of various design methodologies is a subset of the more general problem of software process methodology during system development. We are currently investigating using Metaview to support software process activities [4].

Metaview can support the generation of interactive graphical tools for methodologies such as structured systems analysis, real-time systems design, and structured design. What is not represented currently in these tools, however, is a way of specifying how the development process should proceed (i.e., the methodology of design) in conjunction with tool use. We are therefore investigating how "methodology knowledge" can be modeled and incorporated into the Metaview generated environments – that is, we want to generate "smart" tools. One approach is examining how methodology knowledge can be incorporated into ETL and ECL (Environment Constraint Language), our language for specifying consistency and completeness constraints in a software development environment definition. This extension permits the capture of rules governing the order and nature of design steps. Another approach is to formulate a language, based on the modeling of the design process, for expressing methodology knowledge. Such a language should be expressive enough to specify a wide family of methodologies.

Another topic under further investigation deals with aggregation (decomposition). Many design methodologies specify, at best, a semi-formal way of how decomposition should be performed. Two important aspects of decomposition that we hope to characterize in a general way are how it should be represented and how it should be enacted. The relationship between decomposition and composition is also being examined.

Acknowledgement: We wish to thank Germinal Boloix, Piotr Findeisen, Beth Protsko, and Dinesh Gadwal for their invaluable discussion and contributions to this work. The authors wish to acknowledge the financial support of this work through IRIS Project which is part of the Canadian Federal Networks of Centres of Excellence Program.

References

[1]   V. Arora, J.E. Greer, J.P. Tremblay. *A Framework for Capturing Design Rationale Using Granularity Hierarchies.* Proceedings of fifth International workshop on computer-aided software engineering. Montreal, Canada, 246-251, July 1992.

[2]   G. Babin, F. Lustman, and P. Shoval. *Specification and Design of Transactions in Information Systems: A Formal Approach.* IEEE Transactions on Software Engineering, 17(8):814-829, August 1991.

[3]   G. Boloix, P.G. Sorenson, J.P. Tremblay. *Software Metrics Using a Metasystem Approach to Software Specifications.* Journal of Systems and Software, (20):273-294, 1993.

[4]   G. Boloix, P.G. Sorenson, J.P. Tremblay. *Process Modeling Using a Metasystem Approach to Software Specifications.* Technical Report TR92-11, Department of Computing Science, University of Alberta, September 1992.

[5]   G. Boloix, P.G. Sorenson, J.P. Tremblay. *On Transformations Using a Metasystem Approach to Software Development.* Software Engineering Journal, 7:425-437, 1992.

[6]   R.N. Britcher and J.J. Craig. Using Modern Design Practices to Update Aging Software Systems. IEEE Software, 3(3):16–24, March 1986.

[7]   M. Chen, and J.F. Nunamaker Jr. *MetaPlex: an integrated environment for organization and information systems development,* Proc. Tenth Int'l Conf. on Information Systems, Boston, Dec. 4-6, 1989, pp. 141-151.

[8]   P.P. Chen. *The Entity-Relationship Model - Toward a Unified View of Data.* ACM Transactions on Database Systems, 1:9-36, March 1976.

[9]   J.M. DeDourek, P.G. Sorenson, and J.P.Tremblay. *Metasystems for Information Processing System Specification Environments.* INFOR, 27(3):311-337, August 1989.

[10]   R.G. Fichman and C.F. Kenerer. *Object-Oriented and Conventional Analysis and Design Methodologies: Comparison and Critique.* IEEE Computer, 25(10):22-39, October 1992.

[11]   A.P.J. Jarczyk, P. Loffler and F. M. Shipman. *Design Rationale for Software Engineering: A Survey.* Proceedings of 25th Hawaii International Conference on System Sciences, 577-586, January 1992.

[12]   J.K. Lee. *Implementing ADISSA Transformations in the Metaview Metasystem.* M.Sc. Thesis, Department of Computing Science, University of Alberta, Sept. 1992.

[13]   J. Martin. *System Design from Provably Correct Constructs.* Prentice-Hall, 1985.

[14]   J. Martin and C. McClure. *Design Techniques for Analysts and Programmers.* Prentice-Hall, 1985.

[15]   A.J. McAllister. *Modeling Concepts for Specification Environments.* PhD thesis, Department of Computational Science, Univ. of Saskatchewan, 1988.

[16]   D.R. McCarthy and U. Dayal. *The Architecture of an Active Data Base Management System.* Proc. of 1989 ACM-SIGMOD Int'l Conf., SIGMOD Record 18, 215–224, 1989.

[17]   H. Müller. *Verifying Software Quality Criteria using an Interactive Graph Editor.* Tech. Rep. DCS-139-IR, Dept. of Computer Science, Univ. of Victoria, 1990.

[18]   M. Page-Jones. *The Practical Guide to Structured Systems Design.* Yourdon Press, 1988.

[19]   C. Potts. *A Generic Model for Representing Design Methods.* Proceedings of 11th International Conference on Software Engineering, IEEE Computer Society Press, 217-220, May 1989.

[20]   L.B. Protsko, P.G. Sorenson, J.P. Tremblay, and D.A. Schaefer. *Towards the Automatic Generation of Software Diagrams.* IEEE Transactions on Software Engineering, 17(1):10-21, January 1991.

[21]   K. Smolander, K. Lyytinen, V.P.Tahvanainen and P. Martiin. *MetaEdit: A Flexible Graphical Environment for Methodology Modeling,* Advanced Information System Engineering: Third Int'l Conf. of CAiSE'91, Springer-Verlag, May 1991, pp. 168-191.

[22]   P.G. Sorenson, J.P. Tremblay, and A.J. McAllister. *The Metaview System for Many Specification Environments,* IEEE Software, 5(2):30-38, May 1988.

[23]   P.G. Sorenson, J.P. Tremblay, and A.J. McAllister. *The EARA/GI Model for Software Specification Environments.* Technical Report TR91-14, Department of Computing Science, University of Alberta, June 1991.

[24]   J.P. Tremblay and P.G. Sorenson. *The Theory and Practice of Compiler Writing.* McGraw-Hill, 1985.

[25]   T.F.Verhoef, A. ter Hofstede and G.M.Wijers. *Structuring modelling knowledge for CASE shells,* Advanced Information System Engineering: Third Int'l Conf. of CAiSE'91, Springer-Verlag, May 1991, pp. 502-524.

[26]   E. Yourdon and L. Constantine. *Structured Design: Fundamentals of a Discipline of Computer Program and Systems Design.* Prentice-Hall, 1979.

Constructing Software Design Theories and Models

Arthur Ryman

IBM Canada Laboratory, 1150 Eglinton Avenue East
North York, Ontario, Canada, M3C 1H7
ryman@vnet.ibm.com

Abstract. Software design methods are often taught informally and supported by CASE tools that do not make their underlying rules, or *theory*, explicit. The user of such a method is concerned with constructing a *model* of the system being built that satisfies the theory of this method. We suggest that it is useful to make the underlying design theory explicit, and to allow the designer to extend it to more closely describe the system being built. This paper describes 4Thought, a tool for constructing theories and models, which combines conceptual modeling (Entity-Relationship), graphical database visualization (higraphs), and visual logic programming (GraphLog).

1 Introduction

The practicing software engineer is confronted with a wide assortment of software design methods, such as Structured Analysis and Design [DeM79], Jackson System Development [Jac83], and Object Modeling Technique [RBP+91]. Unfortunately, there are many problems associated with the use of these techniques. First, the techniques are usually explained informally and their application in practice is largely a matter of individual taste. Second, there are typically many variants of a given technique but the ways in which they differ is usually unclear. Third, CASE tool support for the techniques is usually very inflexible, and if customization is supported at all, doing so requires considerable expertise in the internals of the tool.

On the other hand, there is a great deal of similarity between most software design methods and the tools that support them. A typical method consists of some small vocabulary of primitive elements, rules for composing them, diagrammatic notation for displaying them, and guidelines for creating them from a set of stated system requirements. Most tools that support these methods are based on a central database of design facts, and provide facilities for textual and graphical entry and reporting, rule checking, and transformation to implementation artifacts.

This essential similarity of many design methods and their associated tools has led several researchers (e.g., ALMA [vLDD+88]) and CASE tool vendors (e.g., Virtual Software Factory by Systematica) to develop the notion of meta-CASE tools that are used to generate a CASE tool set for any given method.

While this approach helps the CASE tool supplier, it does not help the CASE tool user, since the generated tool is as opaque and inflexible as usual.

We propose that the underlying formalism of any design method should be explicit, accessible, and extendible by the designer, and that the way to accomplish this is to provide CASE tools that treat the formalism as input data. This notion can be expressed in terms of mathematical logic. Mathematicians create *theories* that specify concepts, and the rules, or axioms, they must satisfy. A structure that satisfies the axioms is called a *model* for the theory. Conventional design methods and CASE tools treat system construction exclusively as model-building for their implicit theories. We believe that system construction also has an explicit theory-building component, and we refer to this view of the designer's role as the *Theory-Model Paradigm* [Rym89, RLJ91]. The remainder of this paper describes an approach to constructing software design theories and models, examples of its use, and tools that support it.

2 Entity-Relationship Modeling

The extent to which a design method is formalized depends on the intended use of its models. The designer must therefore determine what aspects of the design to record. The first step in formalizing the method is to create an Entity-Relationship (ER) model [Che76] of the relevant design concepts. These form the primitive concepts of the theory. In general, the semantics of the ER model will not be sufficient to describe the theory. The ER model must therefore be augmented with integrity constraints that correspond to the axioms of the theory.

In addition to forming the basis of the theory, the ER model also suggests how to visualize models as graphs: entities become nodes and relationships become (labeled) arcs. This prescription allows us to associate a semantic network with each model of the theory. In practice, many theories include relationships that define part hierarchies, in which case it is often useful to render the relationship using nesting of nodes within nodes as in Venn diagrams. This gives the semantic network the structure of a higraph.

3 GraphLog

To complete the theory, the designer must specify how any derived concepts are defined in terms of the primitive concepts. To facilitate the construction of models, the designer must specify operations. These are either queries that define useful views of the model, or transactions that define how a model can be updated while preserving the integrity constraints.

The integrity constraints, definitions, queries, and transactions of the theory can be expressed using a formal notation (we use Z [Spi92]). However, given our bias towards thinking of the database as a graph there is a superior alternative: GraphLog [CMR92]. We have observed that we rarely use the full expressive power of predicate calculus in describing typical design methods. The subset we do need turns out to be equivalent to relational algebra with transitive closure, since in practice we only encounter linearly recursive logical formulae. This observation has also been made in the deductive database community [CGT91]. In addition, the relational algebra expressions we encounter correspond to regular expressions [O'K90] that have a natural graphical interpretation in terms of subgraph matching and path traversal. GraphLog is a formal visual logic programming notation that lets us express typical predicate calculus expressions graphically.

4   4Thought

We are building a prototype tool called 4Thought [Rym92], which supports this graphical framework for the Theory-Model paradigm. 4Thought lets the designer connect to a Prolog database server and create workspaces that contain a theory (ER model, and GraphLog definitions, constraints, queries, and transactions) and snapshots (materialized views) of the model stored in the database. The designer can graphically edit the theory and the model, verify the model by checking the integrity constraints, search the model, and generate snapshots of it. These functions are performed by Prolog programs that are automatically generated from the GraphLog modules of the theory.

In the following example, we'll describe how a designer would use 4Thought to construct a design theory about good object-oriented program style. The elements of GraphLog will be described as they are introduced, and recorded using Z notation.

5   The Law of Demeter

The Law of Demeter [LH89] proposes restrictions on how member functions call each other. These restrictions are intended to reduce coupling between classes and improve the understandability of member functions. The law is language-independent, but in the following discussion we will use C++ terminology and examples.

Informally, the law states that a member function should only call other member functions that belong to the classes of its member variables, its arguments, the objects it constructs, and the global variables it accesses.

To formalize this, we must first construct an ER model of the structure of C++ programs. The model we use is a subset of the model used by the IBM AIX XL C++ Browser [IBM92], which uses static analysis information encoded as Prolog facts that are generated by the XL C++ compiler. The complete model is described in [JY92]. Prolog definitions of the Law of Demeter are given in [JMN+92].

The primitive C++ concepts used in the statement of the Law of Demeter are illustrated in Figure 1. Not shown in the figure are relationship set cardinalities and entity set classification relations. The complete semantics of the ER model are given in the *Program* Z schema.

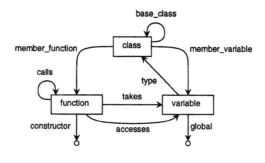

[htbp]

Fig. 1. ER Diagram of Object-Oriented Program Structure

We introduce a basic type, *ENTITY*, from which program entities are drawn:

$$[ENTITY]$$

The C++ program entity sets that we are concerned with are classes, functions, and variables. It is useful to assign them the same type, since they participate in shared relations. For example, classes and functions both define scopes, and functions and variables are both members of classes. However, in the following discussion this sort of shared relation does not occur and it is useful to introduce names for each entity set:

$$CLASS == ENTITY$$
$$FUNCTION == ENTITY$$
$$VARIABLE == ENTITY$$

The formal meaning of Figure 1, augmented with relationship cardinalities and entity classification information is as follows:

```
┌─ Program ─────────────────────────────────────────────
│  class : P CLASS
│  function : P FUNCTION
│  variable : P VARIABLE
│  constructor : P FUNCTION
│  global : P VARIABLE
│  base_class : CLASS ↔ CLASS
│  member_function : CLASS ↔ FUNCTION
│  member_variable : CLASS ↔ VARIABLE
│  calls : FUNCTION ↔ FUNCTION
│  takes : FUNCTION ↔ VARIABLE
│  accesses : FUNCTION ↔ VARIABLE
│  type : VARIABLE ↠ CLASS
├───────────────────────────────────────────────────────
│  disjoint ⟨class, function, variable⟩
│
│  constructor ⊆ function
│  global ⊆ variable
│
│  base_class ∈ class ↔ class
│  member_function~ ∈ function ↠ class
│  member_variable~ ∈ variable ↠ class
│
│  calls ∈ function ↔ function
│  takes~ ∈ variable ↠ function
│  accesses ∈ function ↔ variable
│  type ∈ variable ↠ class
└───────────────────────────────────────────────────────
```

We use the example program given in [LH89] as a model for our theory of program structure (see Figure 2).

The example program was analyzed by the compiler and loaded into a Prolog database. Figure 3 shows a GraphLog query and the resulting snapshot of the database. The query is a filter that only passes the *member_function* and *member_variable* relations, and displays them as a higraph.

We will now state the definitions used in the Law of Demeter, and then give the GraphLog translations of some of them.

5.1 Law of Demeter Definitions

A member function M is a *client* of a class C if M calls a member function F of C or accesses a member variable V of C. A class C is a *supplier* of a member function M if M is a client of C.

A class $C1$ is an *argument class* of a member function M if M takes a variable V of type C or M is a member function of C, and $C1$ is C or a direct or indirect base class of C. (Recall that M takes an implicit argument **this** of type C.)

A class $C1$ is an *instance variable class* of a class $C2$ if $C2$ has a member variable V of type C, and $C1$ is C or a direct or indirect base class of C.

[htbp]

```
typedef int boolean;

class Book{int id;};

class BookSec{public: boolean search(Book *book){return 0;}};

class Documents{public: boolean search(Book *book){return 0;}};

class MicroficheFiles{public: boolean search(Book *book){return 0;}};

class Archive{public:
    MicroficheFiles *arch_microfiche;
    Documents *arch_docs;
    boolean search_good_style(Book *book){
        return (arch_microfiche->search(book) ||
            arch_docs->search(book));
    }
};

class ReferenceSec{public:
    Archive *archive;
    BookSec *ref_book_sec;
    boolean search_bad_style(Book *book){
        return (ref_book_sec->search(book) ||
        /**/    archive->arch_microfiche->search(book) ||
        /**/    archive->arch_docs->search(book));
    }
    boolean search_good_style(Book *book){
        return (ref_book_sec->search(book) ||
            archive->search_good_style(book));
    }
};
```

Fig. 2. Listing of Example C++ Program

A class $C1$ is an *acquaintance* of a member function M of class $C2$ if $C1$ is a supplier of M and is neither an argument class of M nor an instance variable class of $C2$.

A class C is a *preferred acquaintance* of a member function M if C is an acquaintance of M, and M calls a constructor F of C or accesses a global variable V of type C.

A class B is a *preferred supplier* of a member function M of class C if B is a supplier of M, and B is an instance variable class of C or an argument class of M or a preferred acquaintance of M.

The strict version of the class form of the Law of Demeter states that all member functions should have only preferred suppliers.

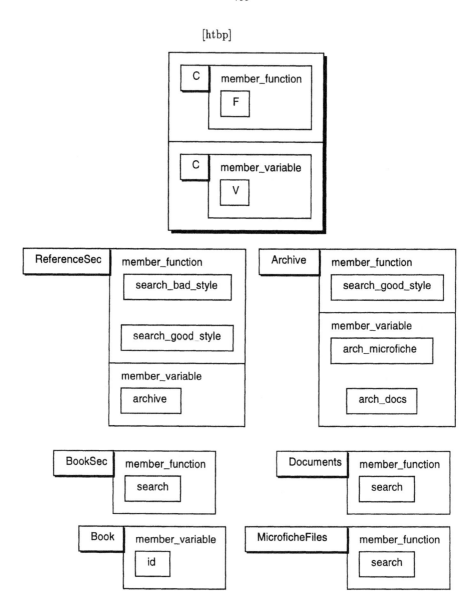

Fig. 3. GraphLog Query and Snapshot of Member Functions and Variables

5.2 Supplier

The GraphLog definition of *client* and *supplier* is illustrated in Figure 4.

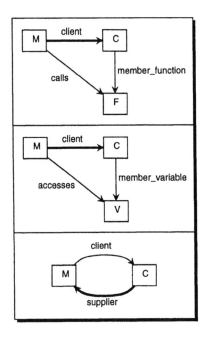

[htbp]

Fig. 4. GraphLog Definition of Client and Supplier

The formal meaning of Figure 4 is as follows:

$\underline{\text{Supplier}}$

Program

$client : FUNCTION \leftrightarrow CLASS$

$supplier : CLASS \leftrightarrow FUNCTION$

$client = (\,calls \,\mathring{\,,}\, member\_function^{\sim}\,) \cup (\,accesses \,\mathring{\,,}\, member\_variable^{\sim}\,)$

$supplier = client^{\sim}$

5.3 ArgumentClass

The GraphLog definition of *argument_class* is illustrated in Figure 5.

The formal meaning of Figure 5 is as follows:

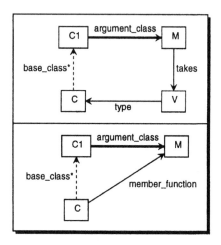

[htbp]

Fig. 5. GraphLog Definition of Argument Class

┌─ *ArgumentClass* ────────────────────────────────────
│ *Program*
│ $argument\_class : CLASS \leftrightarrow FUNCTION$
├──
│ $argument\_class = (base\_class^*)^\sim \,\r{9}\,((takes\,\r{9}\,type)^\sim \cup member\_function)$
└──

5.4 Acquaintance

The GraphLog definitions of *instance_variable_class*, *preferred_acquaintance*, and *preferred_supplier*, along with their corresponding Z schemas, are analogous and will be omitted due to lack of space.

The GraphLog definition of *acquaintance* is illustrated in Figure 6.
The formal meaning of Figure 6 is as follows:

┌─ *Acquaintance* ─────────────────────────────────────
│ *Supplier*
│ *ArgumentClass*
│ *InstanceVariableClass*
│ $acquaintance : CLASS \leftrightarrow FUNCTION$
├──
│ $acquaintance = (supplier \setminus argument\_class) \cap$
│ $\qquad ((id\ class \setminus instance\_variable\_class)\,\r{9}\,member\_function)$
└──

Figure 7 illustrates a GraphLog query that displays the *acquaintance* relation in the context of the *calls* and *member_function* relations, and the resulting snapshot for the example program. Note that `search_bad_style` in `ReferenceSec`

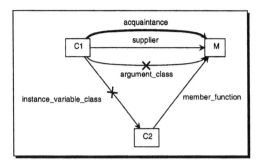

[htbp]

Fig. 6. GraphLog Definition of Acquaintance

has two acquaintance classes (`MicroficheFiles` and `Documents`, as a consequence of its directly calling `search` in `MicroficheFiles` and `Documents`), while `search_good_style` has none.

Lieberherr [LH89] has shown that any program can be transformed into one that satisfies the Law of Demeter, and defines two transformations, *lifting* and *pushing*, for accomplishing this. These transformations could also be expressed as GraphLog transactions, and would allow the designer to graphically edit the design database by direct manipulation of the snapshots. In this mode of working, changes to the base relations would automatically cause corresponding changes to the derived relations, giving the designer immediate feedback and allowing the assessment of different alternatives.

6   Conclusion

We have shown how 4Thought, through its support of conceptual modeling, graphical database visualization, and visual logic programming, provides a framework for constructing theories and models of software design. We believe that the expressive power of GraphLog is adequate for the description of typical software engineering problems, and that its visual character often illuminates equivalent formal text.

In order to make 4Thought a production tool, we need to improve performance in two areas. First, the GraphLog to Prolog translator [Fuk91] needs optimization so that large models can be processed efficiently. Second, we need to incorporate incremental recomputation techniques so that snapshots can be refreshed quickly in response to transactions. Fortunately, both these areas are the subject of active research in the deductive database community.

[htbp]

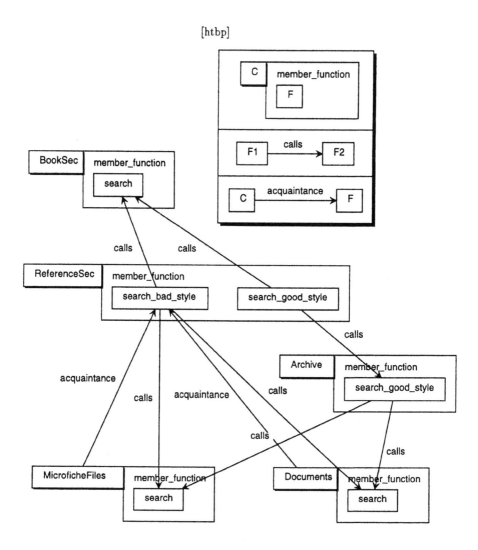

Fig. 7. GraphLog Query and Snapshot of Member Functions, Calls, and Acquaintance

References

[CGT91]   S. Ceri, G. Gottlob, and L. Tanca. Datalog: A self-contained tutorial (part 2). *Programmirovanie (Russia) Program. Comput. Softw. (USA)*, 17(5), September-October 1991.

[Che76]   Peter Chen. The entity relationship model: Towards a unified view of data. *ACM Transactions on Database Systems*, 1(1):9–36, March 1976.

[CMR92]   Mariano Consens, Alberto Mendelzon, and Arthur Ryman. Visualizing and querying software structures. In *Proceedings of the 14th International Conference on Software Engineering*, Melbourne, Australia, May 1992.

[DeM79]   Tom DeMarco. *Structured Analysis and System Specification*. Prentice-Hall, Inc., Englewood Cliffs, New Jersey, 1979.

[Fuk91]   Milan Fukar. Translating Graphlog into Prolog. Technical Report TR 74.080, IBM, October 1991.

[IBM92]   IBM, North York, Ontario. *AIX XL C++ Compiler/6000 User's Guide Version 1*, first edition, April 1992.

[Jac83]   Michael A. Jackson. *System Development*. Prentice-Hall International, 1983.

[JMN+92]   Shahram Javey, Kin'ichi Mitsui, Hiroaki Nakamura, Tsuyoshi Ohira, Kazu Yasuda, Kazushi Kuse, Tsutomu Kamimura, and Richard Helm. Architecture of the xl C++ browser. In John Botsford, Arthur Ryman, Jacob Slonim, and David Taylor, editors, *Proceedings of the 1992 CAS Conference, Volume I*, pages 369–379, Toronto, Ontario, November 1992.

[JY92]   S. Javey and K. Yasuda. The conceptual model for the C++ program database. Technical Report TR 74.093, IBM, May 1992.

[LH89]   Karl J. Lieberherr and Ian M. Holland. Assuring good style for object-oriented programs. *IEEE Software*, pages 38–48, September 1989.

[O'K90]   Richard A. O'Keefe. *The Craft of Prolog*. The MIT Press, Cambridge, Massachusetts, 1990.

[RBP+91]   James Rumbaugh, Michael Blaha, William Premerlani, Frederick Eddy, and William Lorensen. *Object-Oriented Modeling and Design*. Prentice-Hall, Inc., Englewood Cliffs, New Jersey, 1991.

[RLJ91]   Arthur Ryman, David Alex Lamb, and Nitin Jain. Theories and models in software design. Technical Report TR 74.081, IBM, October 1991.

[Rym89]   Arthur Ryman. The theory-model paradigm in software design. Technical Report TR 74.048, IBM, October 1989.

[Rym92]   Arthur Ryman. Foundations of 4Thought. In John Botsford, Arthur Ryman, Jacob Slonim, and David Taylor, editors, *Proceedings of the 1992 CAS Conference, Volume I*, pages 133–155, Toronto, Ontario, November 1992.

[Spi92]   J.M. Spivey. *The Z Notation: A Reference Manual*. Prentice-Hall International (UK) Ltd., London, England, second edition, 1992.

[vLDD+88] Axel van Lamsweerde, Bruno Delcourt, Emmanuelle Delor, Marie-Claire Schayes, and Robert Champagne. Generic lifecycle support in the alma environment. *IEEE Transactions on Software Engineering*, 14(6), June 1988.

Method Integration and Support for Distributed Software Development: An Overview

Jeff Kramer   Anthony Finkelstein   Bashar Nuseibeh

Department of Computing
Imperial College of Science, Technology and Medicine
180 Queen's Gate, London, SW7 2BZ, UK
Email: {jk, acwf, ban}@doc.ic.ac.uk

Abstract. Our main objective is to develop an integrated methodology and associated support tools for the development and management of distributed software systems. Our use of the term "distributed software development" is deliberately ambiguous as it is intended to cover both the development of distributed software and distributed development of software by teams of personnel. This paper overviews our work on methods such as the Constructive Design Approach and integration frameworks such as ViewPoints, but, in the interests of brevity, makes no attempt to compare it with current related work.

1. Objectives and Overview

The key feature of our approach to software development is its emphasis on configuration structure, where "...the notion of the system as a configuration of modular software and hardware components is used as the framework on which to hang the research work on system specification, analysis, construction and modification" [9]. In particular, software systems are described and constructed as configurations of interacting software components. We believe that this emphasis on configuration structure leads to clear and flexible designs, and produces distributed object-based systems which are comprehensible and maintainable. The structural view is particularly useful in facilitating change and evolution in the form of dynamic configuration.

Another feature of the work is its support for multiparadigm approaches. This is reflected in its support for multiple specification and analysis techniques, for the integration of multiple methods and implementation on multiple platforms. A range of techniques and methods have been developed, supporting both formal and informal methods, and permitting top-down and/or bottom-up development. For instance, formal development utilises formal specifications to provide a sound basis for checking system consistency, predicting timing behaviour and assisting in system modification. System construction is then based on the system specification. Alternatively systems can be constructed using an informal but rigorous constructive approach. Specification and method integration is provided through the use of a novel approach, called ViewPoints, which permits supports specification and method partitioning and interaction through explicit transformations analogous to those used in software configurations.

CDA - informal but rigorous

The Constructive Design Approach (Figure-1) [10] is based on the principles of explicit system structure and context independent components. The initial step of the workplan involves the identification of the main processing components of the system and the data flows between them. This gives rise to a structural description of the system in terms of a configuration of processes, with interfaces giving the types of data flows. From this, component types can be identified. A more precise specification of a component interface is then obtained by introducing control information to the data flows. Finally, a component can be elaborated either by hierarchical decomposition into sub-components, or, in the case of a primitive component, by detailed description of its behaviour in a programming language. These method steps are summarised in the diagram below. Although described and shown top-down, the method actually supports and emphasises the more rigorous, constructive (bottom-up) process which is more amenable to analysis and validation. The top-down decomposition process is more informal.

Wanda - formal

Wanda [19] is a formal specification language for the description of parallel time-critical systems. Decompositional design and hierarchical system construction are the techniques of system development supported by Wanda. Component declaration and composition of systems as sets of co-operating instances of components are the basic constructs of system specification. Wanda thus utilises the system development method, CDA, described above. The formal framework of Wanda is adapted from the Timed CSP model, which is embedded into a typed logic language. Timed CSP provides a well understood and widely accepted model of concurrency, communication, and time. The logic language supports this model with a powerful set of data and control abstractions.

The principal new feature of Wanda is the ability to incorporate the specification of the dynamic behaviour of a system component as part of the component type information. On the basis of this type information two well-formedness rules have been defined which permit static checking of correctness of system construction (composition and decomposition) with respect to the specification of the dynamic behaviour.

2.2 Method Integration: ViewPoints

Large system development projects typically consist of a number of participants, engaging in the partial specification of system components. These participants frequently employ different notations and development strategies to produce descriptions of different (or the same) problem domains. To model this scenario we define a ViewPoint [5, 11, 15] as a loosely coupled, locally managed distributable object, encapsulating partial knowledge about the system and domain, specified in a particular, suitable representation scheme, and partial knowledge about the process of development. A ViewPoint encapsulates this knowledge in five so-called slots: style, work plan, domain, specification and work record. These are shown in Figure-2.

Each ViewPoint is associated with a particular development participant called the ViewPoint "owner". The ViewPoint owner is responsible for enacting the ViewPoint work plan to produce a ViewPoint specification, in the ViewPoint style, for the owner's domain of responsibility.

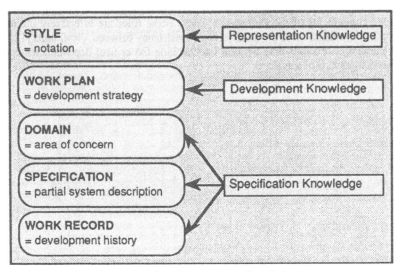

Figure-2: The five slots of a ViewPoint.

Clearly, a number of ViewPoints may employ the same style (e.g., functional decomposition) and the same work plan (e.g., description of a top-down strategy), to produce different specifications for different domains. We therefore define a reusable ViewPoint Template in which only the style and work plan slots are elaborated. A ViewPoint template is in effect a ViewPoint type, whereby a single ViewPoint template may be instantiated to yield several different ViewPoints, and by extension several ViewPoint specifications (Figure-3).

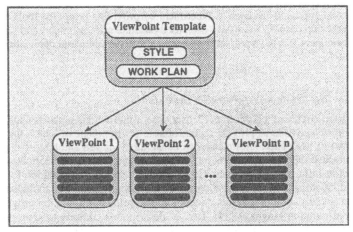

Figure-3: ViewPoints are created by instantiating ViewPoint templates.

A software engineering method in this context is a collection of ViewPoint templates, representing the constituent development techniques of the method (Figure-4). Customised methods, or combinations of methods, may thus be constructed by grouping together the relevant templates. The binding of these templates is via Inter-ViewPoint rules that relate the style components of the various templates. These rules are effectively the method integration mechanism, and are used to check consistency between ViewPoints [17]. Such inter-ViewPoint relations may be used for checking the critical dependencies between various components of a system.

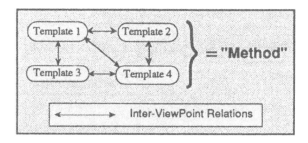

Figure-4: A software engineering method is a structured collection of ViewPoint templates, integrated via a series of inter-ViewPoint relations.

ViewPoint templates are also strong candidates for reuse. One or more such templates may be used in different methods, and because they have been tried and tested, their reuse should lead to more effective and robust methods.

3. Tool Support

The general approach has been to experiment by providing prototype tools to support and realise the approaches. These have been used on small scale examples and case studies by their developers, but have not yet been used on realistic industrial applications nor by external users.

3.1 CDA: *the System Architect's Assistant*

The System Architect's Assistant [13] is a design tool which supports CDA (Figure-5). Its main objective is to provide a comfortable environment in which the software structure and its associated information can be captured viewed and modified easily and quickly. It allows the software structure to be displayed in various formats to enable analysis from different perspectives. Comprehensive support is provided for diagram editing and layout, as well as navigation within the design space. The tool also supports the automatic translation of a design diagram into a partial configuration program in the Darwin configuration language [14]. Darwin descriptions compile to C++ procedures which elaborate the required structures at system generation/instantiation time. Darwin permits the definition of both static and dynamically changing structures. Darwin is neutral with respect to the form of inter-component communication or interface specification used although it will allow these interfaces to be checked for compatibility. The intention is thus to support the design process through Darwin compilation to execution (Figure-6).

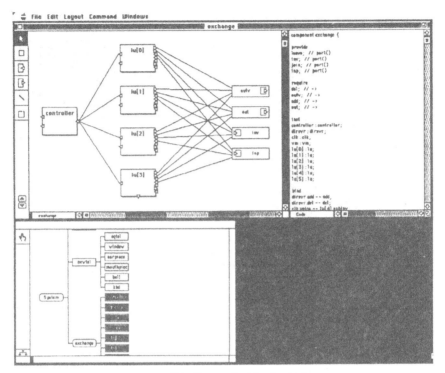

Figure-5: The System Architect's Assistant.

The Architect's Assistant is also to be extended to incorporate other backends to interface with compositional analysis techniques and tools which are compatible with our constructive approach. In this case, the entities being manipulated are not software components but associated attributes giving specifications or models of their functional or timing behaviour. The objective is to ensure that the structure of the system and of its specification is the same. System architects should be free to select those specification techniques that are appropriate to the application. An example of this approach is the work of Castro [1] which uses a form of Petri Nets for the description of individual component behaviour and Causal Temporal Logic for reasoning about composed systems. Zave and Jackson [20] also support the general approach and have recently proposed the use of a simple logic (one-sorted Predicate Logic) to enable the use of "conjunction as composition". This is very promising and seems ideally suited to our framework. Milner's work on the π-calculus is also promising, especially as it has been found to be useful in defining the semantics of Darwin [4]. More recently, the work of Cheung [2, 3] has provided a tractable technique for flow analysis of distributed programs and a technique for compositional analysis of components specified as labelled transition systems.

The SAA is thus intended to act as a front end for specifying the structure and those component specification attributes selected by the designer. It should then be possible to invoke the relevant compositional analysis or verification tools associated with any or all of the provided attributes.

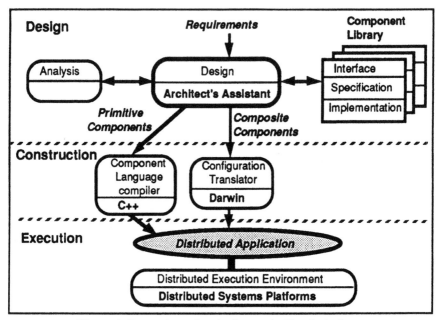

Figure-6: Integration using the System Architect's Assistant.

3.2 ViewPoints: *The Viewer*

The ViewPoint paradigm provides a structural framework for the software development process in a twofold manner. It supports method definition as well as actual system development. The Viewer [16] has been developed as a generic framework tool for both method design and use. It is implemented in Objectworks/Smalltalk .

A "method designer" is provided with the opportunity to design, describe and integrate ViewPoint templates that constitute a method. The constituent techniques of "the method" are chosen, and then a template for each is elaborated. The Viewer provides a Template Browser to facilitate such activities. The consistency relations and transformations between templates of the method are defined under the Inter-ViewPoint Checks section of the work plan.

A "method user" may instantiate pre-defined templates to yield concrete ViewPoints, whose specifications may be developed, checked and managed within the boundaries of a system development project. The Viewer employs a ViewPoint Configuration Browser as the overall project management tool. This browser allows the creation of projects based on pre-defined methods, the instantiation of the methods' constituent templates, and the presentation of selected projects' ViewPoint configuration diagrams.

Actual project development occurs in projects' various constituent ViewPoints using ViewPoint Inspectors (Figure-7). Such tools are loosely coupled and potentially distributable; thus, several ViewPoint Inspectors may be active simultaneously, with different ViewPoint owners developing different ViewPoints concurrently.

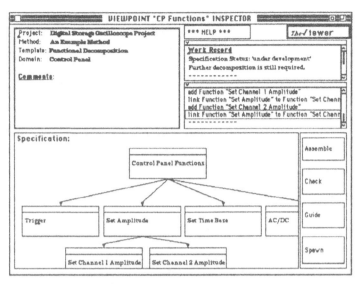

Figure-7: A ViewPoint Inspector. This window provides tools for the development of ViewPoint specifications. These tools include facilities for editing (assembling) specifications and checking their consistency. The diagram shows a "typical" functional decomposition specification, with the work record shown in the two top right window panes.

The ViewPoint Inspector provides the mechanisms for editing and checking ViewPoint specifications - both internally and across other ViewPoints. Editing commands appear under the "Assemble" button and are derived from the "Assembly Actions" description in the corresponding ViewPoint template. Consistency checking may be performed by a rudimentary Consistency Checker (Figure-8), and fine-grain, context-sensitive method guidance is also available [18]. The work record automatically keeps track of all actions performed on the specification, and the user may optionally annotate some or all of these actions to explain or provide a rationale for various design decisions.

Others are also experimenting with the use of ViewPoints. For instance, HyperView is an experimental tool tailored for the use of a particular method [7, 8]. The tool incorporates two paradigms: the ViewPoint paradigm for structured distributed system development and the hypertext paradigm for overall management and organisation of self-contained ViewPoints. The hypertext paradigm provides the means for referencing other ViewPoints when working within one. ViewPoint method and work record status information is handled uniformly in sub-windows which open upon demand. There also is a facility to assign comments or notes to a ViewPoint to explain design decisions or record remarks and annotations to the design. ViewPoint management supports ViewPoint instantiation or deletion, establishing or solving of relations between ViewPoints, clearing, copying, save or reset of ViewPoint contents, handling sub-windows (property sheets, help windows), and tool-related functions (general window handling, sub-window handling, printing of ViewPoints, and setting ViewPoint display modes). The HyperView Tool currently supports the SPEC Net method, based on an extended form of Petri Nets.

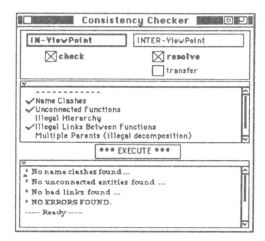

Figure-8: *A ViewPoint Consistency Checker. The scope of the checks is selected first: In- or Inter-ViewPoint. Inter-ViewPoint checks have two modes of application: (1) resolve - answers 'success' or 'fail' when checks are executed, (2) transfer - passes on the necessary information to and/or from other Viewpoints to maintain inter-ViewPoint consistency. The list of appropriate checks is displayed and may be selected and executed individually or in groups.*

4. Future Work

Methods are treated as a union of ViewPoint templates, and method tool support as the union of the individual tools supporting the methods' constituent templates. Tool integration is a natural consequence of the method integration provided by the VOSE framework via inter-ViewPoint relations and transformations. Further work is needed to explore how these relations and transformations should be described and used.

Work on integration of methods, notations and tools has generally been performed by the use of a common data model, usually supported by a common, centralised data base. This has some advantages in providing a uniform basis for consistency checking. Multiple views can still be supported by the provision of mappings to/from the data model. However, we believe that the general use of centralised data repositories is a mistake for the long term. General data models are difficult to design and tend to be even more difficult to modify and extend when new tools are to be integrated. This is analogous to the search for some universal formalism and is reminiscent of the search for a "Holy Grail". Therefore, although this approach has enabled us to make good progress in the provision of current CASE tools, we believe that it is too tightly integrated, especially in its centralised form. It will be one of the major restrictions in the provision of tools which integrate more methods and notations, cover a larger part of the life cycle and support use by large teams of software engineers.

One of the drawbacks cited for such distribution is the problem of consistency. It is generally more difficult to check and maintain consistency in a distributed environment. On the other hand, we believe that we should re-examine this obsession with consistency, and perhaps make more provision for inconsistency [12]. Inconsistency is inevitable as part of the development process. Forcing consistency tends to restrict the development process and stifle novelty and invention. Furthermore, if consistency is required at all times, it can even slow the tool support. Consistency is a relative notion, and should be considered as a piecemeal process, to be checked between particular parts or views of a design or specification. It should only be checked at particular stages rather than enforced as a matter of course. For instance, it does not seem necessary or desirable that all entities in a system be uniformly named, provided that transformations and mappings between the names in different views are eventually provided. We are investigating techniques for inconsistency handling which do not enforce consistency and which permit actions to be associated with particular inconsistencies [6].

Method guidance is another area in which we hope to contribute. Methods are systems of recommended procedures and are intended to supplement rather than replace an analyst's skill. Advice should be provided to support normal use of the method. However, a support tool that could not deal with deviations from the recommended method and treated them as 'errors' from which it could not recover, would be unacceptable. A crucial part of any active guidance system for a requirements method is the remediation mechanism whereby possible repair procedures are deduced and recommended to the practitioner. In addition, the guidance system should include some ordering or prioritisation of advice between alternative actions, such as corrective actions before method steps.

Finally, our research is also focused on improving the structuring of large ViewPoint configurations [11] to allow the scaling up of the framework to large, industrial developments. Moreover, a variety of notations and mechanisms for expressing and implementing inter-ViewPoint communication in a distributed environment are also being investigated [17].

5. Impact on Industrial Practice

We believe that our work will impact industrial practice in a number of ways:

1. *CDA emphasises the importance of the structural (configuration) view and its central role in systems development.*

Although most designers constantly use such architectural diagrams to define and discuss their work, few methods specify and retain that structure through the method steps, using it as the main reference and framework for later steps. This configuration approach lends itself to support by both graphical and textual tools to facilitate human design and interpretation as well as machine processing and translation into actual systems.

2. *ViewPoint oriented systems engineering acknowledges the inevitable role played by a multitude of development techniques in a single development project.*

ViewPoints encapsulate representation, development and specification knowledge within a single object. Further modularity is achieved by selecting ViewPoints that describe different problem domains. ViewPoints are bound together by inter-ViewPoint relations which specify dependencies and mappings (critical or otherwise) between system components. These relations represent the integration thread that passes through the configuration of system ViewPoints, which are otherwise entirely loosely-coupled and locally managed. In addition, its object-based architecture offers considerable scope for reuse. Reuse is supported at the levels of both method design and method use. ViewPoint templates are the reusable components of representation and development knowledge during method design and construction. ViewPoints are the reusable components of specification knowledge during method use.

How can we influence industrial practice? We believe that both these approaches will be shown to be useful and, most importantly, cost effective by their use in larger industrial demonstrators. The combination of industrial experience, tool support and the provision of tutorials and consultant advise can then be combined to convince other industrial users to adopt the approaches, and to encourage commercial tool developers to maintain and further enhance the tool support.

Acknowledgements

Some of the work described in this paper was conducted in the ESPRIT project REX (2080) on "Reconfigurable and Extensible Parallel and Distributed Systems" [9]. We gratefully acknowledge the work of our partners in that project. Current financial support is provided by the DTI in the Advanced Technology Programme of ESF under grant ref.: IED4/410/36/002.

Selected References

1. J. Castro and J. Kramer, "Temporal-Causal System Specification", Proc. of IEEE Int. Conf. on Computer Systems and Software Engineering (CompEuro '90), Israel, May 1990.

2. S.C. Cheung and J. Kramer, "Tractable Flow Analysis for Anomaly Detection in Distributed Programs", Proc. of the 4th European Software Engineering Conference (ESEC '93), Garmisch, Germany, 13-16th Sept. 1993, Springer-Verlag, 283-300.

3. S.C. Cheung and J. Kramer, "Enhancing Compositional Analysis with Interfaces", Technical Report DoC 93/13, Dept. of Computing, Imperial College, April 1993.

4. S. Eisenbach and R. Paterson, "π-Calculus Semantics for the Concurrent Configuration Language Darwin", Proc. of 26th HICSS, Hawaii, January 1993, Software Track, 456-462.

5. A. Finkelstein, J. Kramer, B. Nuseibeh, L. Finkelstein and M. Goedicke, "Viewpoints: a framework for integrating multiple perspectives in system development", International Journal of Software Engineering and Knowledge Engineering , Special Issue on Trends and Directions in Software Engineering Environments, 2 (1), March 1992, 31-58.

6. A. Finkelstein, D. Gabbay, A. Hunter, J. Kramer and B. Nuseibeh, "Inconsistency Handling in Multi-Perspective Specifications", Proc. of the 4th European Software Engineering Conference (ESEC '93), Garmisch, Germany, 13-16th Sept. 1993, Springer-Verlag, 84-99.

7. P. Graubmann, The HyperView Tool Standard Methods, REX technical report REX-WP3-SIE-021-V1.0, Siemens, Munich, Germany, January '92.

8. P. Graubmann, The Petri Net Method ViewPoints in the HyperView Tool, REX technical report REX-WP3-SIE-023-V1.0, Siemens, Munich, January '92.

9. J. Kramer, "Configuration Programming - A Framework for the Development of Distributable Systems", Proc. of IEEE Int. Conf. on Computer Systems and Software Engineering (CompEuro 90), Tel-Aviv, Israel, May 1990, 374-384.

10. J. Kramer, J. Magee and A. Finkelstein, "A Constructive Approach to the Design of Distributed Systems", Proceedings of the 10th International Conference on Distributed Computing Systems, Paris, France, June 1990.

11. J. Kramer and A. Finkelstein, "A Configurable Framework for Method and Tool Integration", Proc. of European Symp. on Software Development Environments and CASE Technology, Konigswinter, Germany, June 1991, Springer-Verlag.

12. J. Kramer, "CASE Support for the Software Process: A Research Viewpoint", Proc. of 3rd European Software Engineering Conference, ESEC, Milan, Oct. 1991, LNCS 550, ed. van Lamsweerde, Fugetta, Springer Verlag 1991.

13. J. Kramer, J. Magee, K. Ng and M. Sloman, "Tool Support for the Design and Construction of Distributed Systems: The System Architect's Assistant", Proc. of 4th IEEE Workshop on Future Trends of Distributed Computing Systems, Lisbon, Sept. 1993, 284-290.

14. J. Magee, J. Kramer and N. Dulay, "Darwin/MP: An Environment for Parallel and Distributed Programming", Proc. of 26th HICSS, Hawaii, January 1993, Software Track, 337-346.

15. B.A. Nuseibeh, VOSE: An Interim Report and Case Study, Internal Report, Department of Computing, Imperial College, March 1991.

16. B. Nuseibeh and A. Finkelstein, "ViewPoints: A Vehicle for Method and Tool Integration", CASE 92, Montreal, Canada, July 1992.

17. B. Nuseibeh, J. Kramer and A. Finkelstein, "Expressing the Relationship between Multiple Views in Requirements Specification", Proc. of 15th IEEE Int. Conf. on Software Engineering (ICSE-15), May 1993, 187-196.

18. B. Nuseibeh, A. Finkelstein and J. Kramer, "Fine-Grain Process Modelling", Proc. of 7th International Workshop on Software Specification and Design (IWSSD-7), Redondo Beach, California, 6-7th December 1993.

19. J. Trescher, "Compositional Specification of Parallel Time-Critical Systems", Proc. of Int. Conf. on Computer Languages, San Francisco, 1992.

20. P. Zave and M. Jackson, "Conjunction as Composition", ACM Transactions on Software Engineering and Methodology, July 1993.

Program Restructuring via Design-Level Manipulation

William G. Griswold and Robert W. Bowdidge

Department of Computer Science & Engineering
University of California, San Diego
La Jolla, CA 92093-0114, U.S.A.
{wgg,bowdidge}@cs.ucsd.edu

Abstract. A meaning-preserving program restructuring tool can be used by a software engineer to change a program's structure to better support modifications during maintenance. Our implementation of such a tool performs restructuring transformations on code fragments that are selected using a text-based interface. However, a text representation does not represent program structure well because some component relationships that we conceptualize as structure are not readily observable in the program text. For example, structural properties such as module uses or procedure calls are represented by references to names rather than by proximity or direct linkage. Since restructuring is primarily a design-oriented activity, this design information must be readily available. Although the program text may be the wrong representation to manipulate, we still want transformations to directly affect the implementation. To solve both these problems, we use a graphical representation of the program design that displays the program's structure and, unlike visualization tools, permits direct manipulation of the structure to perform transformations on the implementation. We introduce a direct manipulation graphical interface that meets these criteria. We describe its design and implementation, and discuss the special problems of direct-manipulation program restructuring at the design level, and relate it to other approaches for manipulating designs.

1 The Problem

Software is perceived to be too expensive relative to its quality. Since maintenance is the dominant phase in the program life-cycle [9], substantially reducing the cost of software requires lowering the cost of maintenance.

As useful software ages, modifications to meet the needs and demands of users are layered upon the original implementation. Modifications unanticipated in the design sometimes are not easily integrated into the existing implementation, requiring changes to multiple modules in the system to complete a single change [12]. As repeated modifications are made, the design and implementation become increasingly less understandable until maintenance becomes unacceptably

---

* This work was supported in part by NSF Grant CCR-9211002.

expensive, and the only solutions are to reimplement the system or restructure it [8].

Restructuring is the more attractive approach. However, it is a complex, program-wide activity that is error-prone when performed manually [5]. Techniques have been described for automatically maintaining the program's consistency as the user manipulates the structure of a program, and a prototype tool for performing meaning-preserving restructuring has been implemented using the techniques [4] [6]. The tool improves the process of making maintenance changes by separating the process into two sequential, independent tasks. The first is to restructure the program, without changing its meaning, into a form that localizes the scope of the modification or otherwise improves the structure to prepare for the modification. The second task is to insert the modification into the restructured program. The meaning-preserving nature of the tool obviates the need to test the restructured program for added errors before proceeding with the modification.

In the prototype tool, which restructures programs written in the imperative programming language Scheme [2], the software engineer manipulates the structure of the program by selecting expressions in the source code as parameters to a restructuring operation (Fig. 1). The primary benefit of restructuring source code is that it is the most familiar and commonly available representation [17]. Also, restructuring the source does not require changing representations between restructuring and modification.

However, manipulating a program's structure through its implementation is inappropriate because manipulating structure is a design issue, not an implementation issue. In particular, the program text contains information that is irrelevant to the manipulation of the structure, and presents the program at a level of detail ill-suited to support modification of the program structure. Also, the software engineer cannot immediately perceive the structure of the program in the program text—it must be carefully inferred. The relation of a variable use or function call to its definition must be identified through references to an address or symbol, rather than through proximity or visible links. Moreover, the implementation displays details that are unrelated to the structure of the system, such as syntax added for readability or the sequence of operations performed by a procedure. For these reasons, restructuring a program by manipulating textual objects is awkward. A representation that better represents structure and design information is needed.

2 Graphical Interfaces for Restructuring

One possible solution is to use a graphical design notation to represent the program. Graphical representations of design are used in many existing tools [10] [13] because the pictorial representation of structure often can convey the needed information in a more readily assimilable manner. A graphical representation can convey program component relationships through direct linkage and grouping, allowing immediate comprehension. A graphical notation also allows the soft-

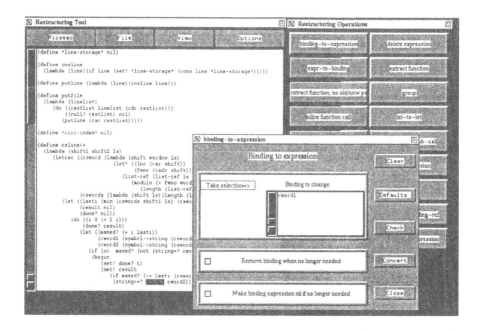

Fig. 1. Text-oriented user interface for Restructuring Tool. The left window contains the program text, and allows selection of expressions within the code. The upper right window contains a button for each possible transformation. When the transformation button is pressed, a panel such as the lower right window appears. To perform a transformation, the user fills in the parameters of the transformation through selection of program text or direct input, then presses the Convert button. When the transformation occurs, the program text window is updated to contain the transformed program.

ware engineer more freedom to choose the relations to be presented, eliding the implementation details that are deemed unnecessary to restructuring, and reducing the number of elements a programmer must examine when performing restructuring operations. A suitable notation can represent objects in a structure familiar to the software engineer. A rich notation also allows information not normally visible to be displayed on top of the structure. For example, variable use between modules might be discouraged in a given methodology; the notation could highlight these instances of high coupling.

Finally, a well-chosen notation can go beyond traditional visualization to allow restructuring transformations to be performed upon the objects underlying the notation. In order for the manipulation of the design notation to cause transformations upon the implementation text, mappings must exist between objects in the notation and the code in the implementation, and transformations on objects in the notation must have mappings to transformations on the implementation. Given these mappings, the feasibility of a restructuring and its precise impacts on the implementation can be known immediately.

3 A Notation for Graphical Restructuring

We have implemented an interface for the restructuring tool that presents a manipulable graphical representation of the program structure.

The graphical notation we chose (see Figs. 2 and 4) is similar to the structure chart notation described in "Structured Design" [16]. We use the notation because it represents many of the objects we intend the user to manipulate, and presents relations necessary for understanding how to restructure a program. The original notation presents functions, call-graph information, and intra-function variable references. Our extensions include objects and relations not represented in the original notation. Parameters to a function are displayed within the function's box to permit their manipulation. A variable reference is displayed in its containing procedure as a separate object, thus allowing the programmer to manipulate either the variable reference or the variable declaration. Modules are also included (in the sense of Common Lisp's packages [15]). Since Scheme's scoping rules allow functions and variables within other functions and modules, such objects are drawn in a nested manner. To assist the tool user in identifying where a variable is referenced, a variable reference is graphically connected with the variable declaration it references.

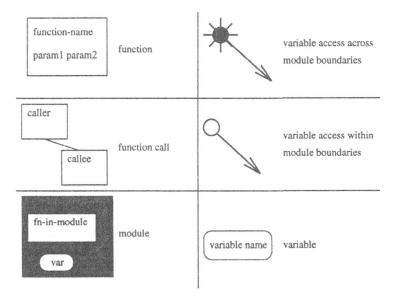

Fig. 2. Our notation for describing structure, derived from "Structured Design" [16]. The variable access symbols exist within functions, and represent variable accesses made by the function. Variable accesses are always graphically connected to the variable they represent.

In addition to specifying structural objects and relations from the source code, the notation used for restructuring can introduce relations and objects that highlight information pertinent to a particular design methodology. For example, in our notation, intra- and inter-module variable references have distinct symbols in order to highlight inter-module variable references, which in some circumstances are unacceptable in a methodology emphasizing data encapsulation.

4 Prototype Design and Implementation

The structure chart is automatically derived from the program text, guaranteeing that the two are always consistent. As the text is parsed into the chart, the tool builds mappings between the text objects and the objects displayed on the screen, which later support mapping transformations on the chart to transformations on the text.

With our prototype user interface, the software engineer can directly manipulate functions, variables, variable references, and modules. An object is renamed by editing its displayed name. Other transformations are applied by the engineer picking-up, dragging, and dropping an object using the workstation's mouse. The transformation performed is chosen in the tool through a table lookup keyed on the type of the object being dragged and the type of the object it is dropped onto. Any information that cannot be inferred from the action is prompted for in a dialog box. The selected transformation is then applied in the text-based transformation tool. When the transformation completes, the structure chart is updated to reflect the changes to the text. Since the tool uses the types of the object being manipulated and the target object to decide which transformation to perform, fewer additional parameters must be explicitly specified to perform a transformation as compared to the text interface (see Fig. 1).

The restructuring tool is written in Allegro Common Lisp, and uses the Picasso Application Framework [14] to implement the graphical user interface portions of the code. The tool runs on a Sun Sparcstation 2 workstation. Currently under development are module-level transformations and data-driven inference of unspecified parameters. Figure 3 shows a black-and-white translation of a color screen image of the structure manipulation interface for the tool.

5 Example

To demonstrate the nature of the design-level restructuring tool, we describe some of the operations that convert a functional decomposition of the KWIC (Key Word In Context) index production program into a data-encapsulated decomposition of the program [12]. (The transformations are described in greater detail in [4]). KWIC takes a text file as input and produces the list of words appearing in the document, with the context of each word (the rest of its enclosing line, circularly shifted to place the keyed word at the beginning of the line) appearing with it.

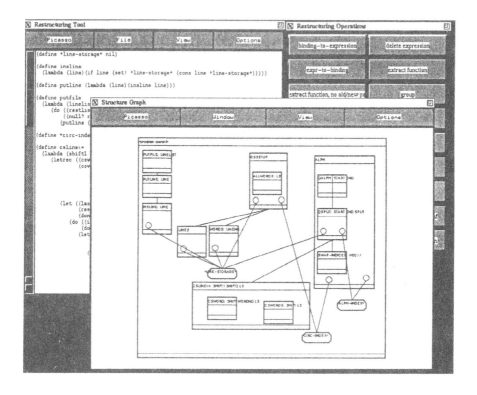

Fig. 3. Structure-oriented graphical user interface for Restructuring Tool. The upper-left window again holds the text representation of the program for reference and manipulation. The window in the center holds a structural view of the system.

Figure 4 presents the structure of KWIC implemented in a functional decomposition. The program represented by this structure is written in Scheme and is about 300 lines long. This version is divided into four modules, each performing a major subtask. The Input module reads lines of text into an internal array, the Circular Shifter module shifts the line's contents to show the keyword followed by the words in context, the Alphabetization module sorts the circular shifts, and the Output module produces the keyword list. Each module shares data with succeeding modules using shared arrays—*line-storage*, *circ-index*, and *alph-index*. Since we are encapsulating data representations, we must eliminate inter-module variable accesses, which are highlighted in our customized version of the notation. Since each module uses the results of previous modules, there are many inter-module variable accesses, and the tool user is visually alerted to these accesses, quickly ascertaining which modules are tightly coupled with respect to representation choice.

It is first noted that *line-storage* is directly accessed by many modules. The first task, then, is to hide the *line-storage* array in its own module. A

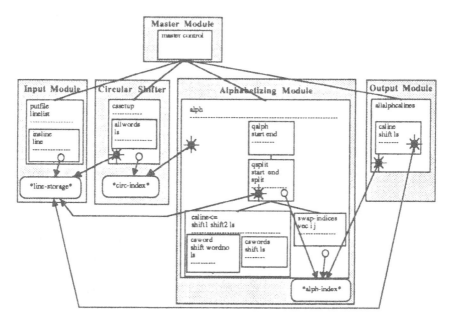

Fig. 4. Functional decomposition of the KWIC indexing program.

new module is created for the line storage by choosing a command from a menu. We then change the module of *line-storage* to the Line Storage module by selecting the *line-storage* variable declaration object and dragging it into the new module. When the transformation is mapped to the text-based restructuring tool, it checks that the modification will not introduce name conflicts or affect dependencies on the variable. The **insline** function (within **putfile**) is strongly related to *line-storage* so it is moved out of **putfile** and into the Line Storage module in the same fashion. Figure 5 shows the structure of the program after these modifications.

The references to *line-storage* within the function **cssetup** are inside common pieces of code that return the number of lines in the array, and the number of words in a given line. These should actually be top level functions. We create the new functions, **lines** and **words**, by dragging a variable reference out of **cssetup** and into its destination, the Line Storage module. The tool then pops up a window containing a text view of **cssetup**, and prompts the user to select the code to be the body and parameters of the new function. The transformation is then performed. Figure 6 shows the new structure.

Further restructuring creates new functions from inlined expressions, inlines array arguments to function calls, and changes the scope of objects. The resulting structure appears in Fig. 7. Not only has the notation aided perceiving the prob-

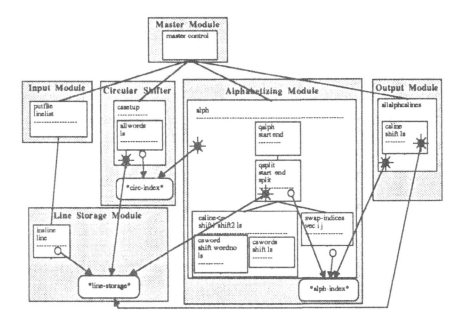

Fig. 5. First step in converting the functional decomposition of the KWIC example from a functional decomposition (Fig. 4) to a data-encapsulated decomposition. (Fig. 7) At this point, the Line Storage module has been created, and the insline function and *line-storage* variable have been moved into it.

lems in KWIC, but the direct manipulations on the notation also restructured the program text in lock step, in the process assuring that the restructuring is feasible and the meaning of the program is unchanged.

6 Limitations of the Current Approach

We find our notation and interface simplify the task of restructuring. However, the current approach and its implementation have a number of limitations, which are topics for current and future research. Three of these limitations are related to manipulating both the design notation and the program text. First, restructuring frequently involves abstracting new design elements from fragments of the program's implementation, such as functions from inlined expressions. To maintain the correspondence between the design and implementation, introducing a new design element such as a function requires linking it to the appropriate code fragment in the implementation. Creating a new function requires either the programmer to specify the code fragment to extract (using a view of the program text), or the restructuring tool to infer the code fragment based upon

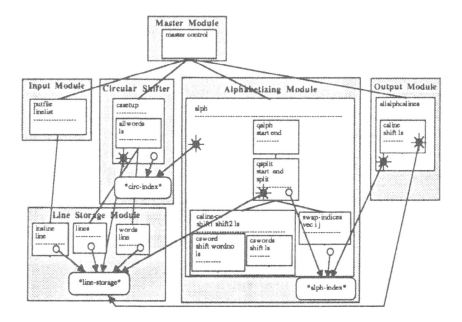

Fig. 6. The accesses to the variable *line-storage* from within cssetup are turned into functions by extracting the expression containing *line-storage* and using that as the body of the new function. The functions can then be moved into the Line Storage module. The last reference to *line-storage* will be extracted at a later step.

objects in the design being manipulated and additional information from the user. If the tool infers the code to extract, the restructuring task can be done completely within the design view, but gives the programmer less control. A solution allowing either approach would be appropriate.

Second, by changing the focus from implementation to design—and text to graphics—some information that might be useful to the software engineer is lost. For example, two functions may be placed close together in the text because they informally share information, such as the algorithm they use. If the functions are placed far apart in the structure chart to produce a cleaner layout, the software engineer may overlook the subtle relationship between the functions. We need more experience to see if this loss causes difficulty for users or if we can eliminate the problem. Other restructuring operations cannot be performed within the structure chart because they are implementation-oriented. For example, converting a **let** scoping construct to a **let*** cannot be handled at the design-level. However, the textual interface properly provides the support for such operations.

The third problem is that currently the design view is derived directly from the text, rather than an independently created design document. So although the

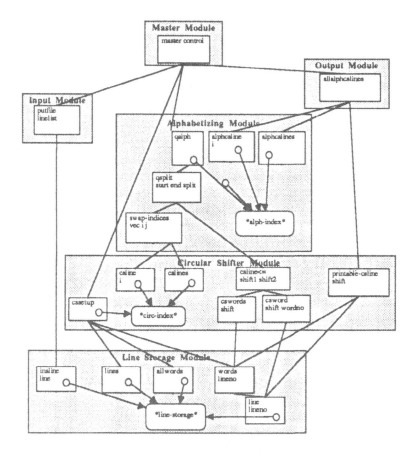

Fig. 7. Data-encapsulated decomposition of the KWIC program. This structure was generated by applying meaning-preserving transformations to the original structure shown in Fig. 4.

tool provides the right level of access, it does not support restructuring through a system's original design document. However, this should be possible for some real design notations, given that the appropriate links can be made between the design and the implementation to allow simultaneous restructuring of the two. The PegaSys system [10] (see Related Work) uses a simple technique for the user to establish links when they cannot be automatically derived.

Finally, since the information in a program is often not projectable into two dimensions, a graphical representation of a program can degrade into a spider web of connecting arcs for larger programs [1], a problem often encountered in program visualization. This problem can be mitigated by techniques such as those used in the Rigi program understanding system, which allows its user to remove extraneous information with elision and tool-assisted grouping of structural [11]. Similarly, automatically generating readable layouts of structure charts is difficult for large programs. Currently the tool uses a simple algorithm for initial layout, then allows the software engineer to interactively improve the layout. The engineer's adjustments then can be used in automatic layout decisions and saved for future restructuring sessions. More sophisticated layout techniques, such as force-directed heuristics [3] can reduce the need for user customization.

7 Related Work

There are many systems that support working graphically with programs. We discuss a few that are most relevant to our work.

The Rigi reverse engineering environment provides semi-automatic construction of system views that assist understanding [11]. Views are initially constructed by the environment and then modified and augmented by the environment user. These additions by the user allow describing the system in abstractions not visible in the implementation. The combination of automatic construction of views, combined with user customization, supports quick construction of views with complete user control. Rigi uses spatial and visual display of information to facilitate rapid understanding. Spatial display reveals contextual relationships, and visual differentiation and connection reveals similarities of components and their non-spatial relationships.

Our techniques benefit from a similar visual model, although ours is currently more primitive. Rigi's ability to augment views can be used in our tool for eliding currently unnecessary detail to provide more space to the part of the system under scrutiny. Rigi's manipulations, however, only augment the external descriptions of the system, not allowing manipulation of the implementation directly. To support manipulation of the underlying program, additional representations must be added to the tool to provide the program text in a manipulable form, and detailed connections between the design and implementation representation are required. Rigi currently only analyzes the text to the extent required to derive the high-level design relationships.

The Garden project [13] notes that programmers benefit from using many notations during design, each view suited to a design technique. The STATEMATE environment, for instance, supports this need by providing physical layout, dataflow, and state machine notations to describe and prototype reactive systems [7]. Garden permits the programmer to define custom textual and graphical notations and describe designs with these notations. Garden then keeps the multiple views of a design consistent with each other as manipulations are performed, and supports limited rule-based execution of the designs to permit testing certain properties.

Garden does not require meaning-preserving transformations or links to the implementation because it focuses on designing new systems, rather than maintaining existing ones. Since no implementation exists in the initial design phase, maintaining correctness of the design only requires comparing the programmer's notion of correctness against the execution of the design. If Garden were used for manipulating the design of existing systems, additional transformations that preserved properties of both the design and implementation might be defined. Garden's observation that multiple design notations are necessary during design suggests a need for multiple notations to aid restructuring in our tool. For example, the notation we use can highlight data-encapsulated structure. Another quality of the design, such as layering, might benefit from a customized notation displaying layering properties.

The PegaSys system is a program analysis system based on visual formalisms [10]. Although the formal verification of program properties is valuable, the work involved in dealing with textual formalisms and relating them to the program implementation is daunting. PegaSys adds a layer of visual formalisms on top of textual ones to speed constructing a description and facilitate understanding. Visually, these formalisms are not unlike the ones provided in Rigi, but are perhaps are at a higher conceptual level. PegaSys also provides a straightforward graphical interface for the tool user to connect the visual formalisms to the implementation. Once the visual formalisms are entered and connected to the implementation, PegaSys can proceed with the verification process.

The formal visual descriptions in PegaSys are basically design elements, and substantially assist program understanding, independent of the additional automation. As with our system, the connection to the implementation provides substantial manipulative power. PegaSys's use of user input to connect design elements to implementation is a technique that we use in our system for transformations that create new abstractions. PegaSys could probably ease the connection task with the semi-automated connection technique supported by Rigi.

A complete system for design-level manipulation of programs should support developing descriptive views, formal analysis, and direct manipulation of the design and implementation in concert. The similar designs of Garden, Rigi, PegaSys, and our system suggest that this integration is possible.

8   Conclusion

Tool-assisted program restructuring can improve the structure of a program to lower the excessively high cost of maintenance. However, a text-based restructuring technique forces the tool user to work with an inappropriate representation of the program. By displaying and restructuring the program at the design level, the software engineer can work directly with the concepts to be manipulated, not their implementation.

Our graphically based restructuring tool promotes understanding and manipulating of these concepts by displaying the structure of the program, directly representing the relations between components, and supporting restructuring through direct manipulation. Customization of the notation allows highlighting structural elements pertinent to a particular design methodology. By linking the design notation with the program text, feedback on the full consequences of a restructuring is immediate. Our prototype demonstrates that high-level, program structural redesign is feasible.

Acknowledgements

We thank David Notkin for discussions on this subject and comments on an earlier draft of this paper. We also thank the Picasso group at the University of California, Berkeley for their help in using the Picasso environment.

References

1. Fredrick P. Brooks Jr. No Silver Bullet: essence and accidents of software engineering. *IEEE Computer*, 20(4):10–19, 1987.
2. R. K. Dybvig. *The Scheme Programming Language*. Prentice-Hall, Englewood Cliffs, NJ, 1987.
3. Peter Eades. A heuristic for graph drawing. *Congressum Numerantium*, 42:149–160, 1984.
4. William G. Griswold. *Program Restructuring to Aid Software Maintenance*. PhD thesis, University of Washington, 1991.
5. William G. Griswold and David Notkin. Computer-aided vs. manual program restructuring. *ACM SIGSOFT Software Engineering Notes*, 17(1), 1992.
6. William G. Griswold and David Notkin. Automated assistance for program restructuring. *Transactions on Software Engineering and Methodology*, 2(3), 1993.
7. David Harel, Hagi Lachover, Amnon Naamad, Amir Pnueli, Michal Politi, Rivi Sherman, Aharon Shtull-Trauring, and Mark Trakhtenbrot. STATEMATE: a working environment for the development of complex reactive systems. *IEEE Transactions on Software Engineering*, 16(4):403–414, 1990.
8. M. M. Lehman and L. A. Belady. *Program Evolution: processes of software change*. Academic Press, London, 1985.
9. B. Lientz and E. Swanson. *Software Maintenance Management: A Study of the Maintenance of Computer Application Software in 487 Data Processing Organizations*. Addison-Wesley, Reading MA, 1980.
10. Mark Moriconi and Dwight F. Hare. Visualizing program designs through PegaSys. *IEEE Computer*, 18(8):72–85, 1985.
11. H. A. Müller, S. R. Tilley, M. A. Orgun, B. D. Corrie, and N. H. Madhavaji. A reverse engineering environment based on spacial and visual software interconnection models. In *Fifth ACM SIGSOFT Symposium on Software Development Environments*, pages 88–98, 1992.
12. D. L. Parnas. On the criteria to be used in decomposing systems into modules. *Communications of the ACM*, 15(12):1053–1058, 1972.
13. Steven P. Reiss. Working in the Garden environment for conceptual programming. *IEEE Software*, 4(6):16–27, 1987.
14. Lawrence A. Rowe, Joseph A. Konstan, Brian C. Smith, Steve Seitz, and Chung Liu. The PICASSO application framework. In *14th ACM Symposium on User Interface Software and Technology*, pages 95–106, 1991.
15. Guy L. Steele Jr. *Common Lisp the Language*. Digital Press, 1990.
16. W. P. Stevens, G. J. Myers, and L. L. Constantine. Structured design. *IBM Systems Journal*, 13(2):115–139, 1974.
17. Mark Weiser. Source code. *IEEE Computer*, 20(11):66–73, 1987.

Hierarchical Modular Diagrams:
An Approach to Describe Architectural Designs

Jorge L. Díaz-Herrera[†]

[†]Software Engineering Institute, Carnegie Mellon University[1]
Pittsburgh, PA 15213-3890

Abstract. A language independent diagrammatic notation for describing the static software structure of an architectural design is introduced. The notation serves to specify the structural relations between the comprising modules and the mapping of design concepts into a hierarchy of actual program components. It can incorporate concepts from other (textual) languages by separating design-oriented syntax, i.e., the notation itself, from detailed "inner" syntax as defined by an underlying textual language. This allows for tools to be built that generate actual code from the specified design structures, and more importantly, that create design structures during reverse engineering in support of reuse. A complete isomorphism is given for existing design languages to illustrate the technique.

1   Introduction

During software description one tries to portray a conceptual design as architectural structures[2] made out of hierarchies of modules representing the various levels and kinds of abstractions. This architecture depicts both dynamic control relations between functional modules, *the dynamic structure*, and static source text relations between encapsulating independent modules, *the static structure*. It is our contention that the static structure plays a crucial role in the management of this usually large collection of software modules, some of which stem from reusable library components, but most are a result of avoiding monolithic systems. (It is simply awkward to try to build a software system as a large piece of linear text). Analyses of large software systems present interesting problems; for example, there is no need to show every 'module' call, instead, clusters indicating visibility requirements would be indispensable.

Our investigations sought to find out how plausible it was to consider static structural concerns early in the design process. We found ourselves in need of a useful (practical) design representation for large software systems, that was not only easy to construct, but more importantly, easy to rebuild during reverse engineering (either for maintenance or reuse purposes), and with the flexibility needed to support several textual design languages. We devised a new diagrammatic technique for this purpose. The notation, Hierarchical Modular Diagrams, or HMD for short, serves to specify the

---

[1.] The majority of this work was done while the author was at George Mason University and was partially supported by George Mason's Center of Excellence for C3I.

[2.] Although the terms "structure" and "architecture" are sometimes used as synonyms, we use the latter to refer to the software dynamic and static structures.

structural relations between the comprising modules and the mapping of design concepts into a hierarchy of actual software components.

The HMD technique is an extension of the Hierarchical Structured Diagrams [2]. The latter was developed to show both structured control flow and refinement steps during program development, suitable for programming-in-the-small. The new HMD technique is a natural evolution of that work, specially suited for programming-in-the-large, addressing higher-level design concerns than those found in simple program development by describing the static relations between modules explicitly. HMD shows import/export relations among modules as well as their top-down decomposition into refinement modules.

Many of the HMD notions discussed below are found in modern software engineering languages such as Ada and Modula-2. What we have done is to incorporate these modern software engineering notions into a language independent, simple and orthogonal graphical form. We demonstrate the usefulness of this approach by providing complete isomorphisms between the HMD technique and other textual design notations.

We have designed HMD thinking on the provision of automated tools, thus the diagrams' outline is quite simple. There is no need for complicated displaying algorithms in order to provide aesthetically pleasing diagrams. Designs tend to grow downwards and to the right of the drawing space. Tools are being built to generate code from HMD designs.

We are also using HMD for reverse engineering and re-engineering. We are experimenting with a clustering algorithm to help us identify "components" from a collection of Ada library units (a form of reverse engineering) in support of design-for-reuse. Component-based software development refers to the capability to integrate a coherent working system out of a collection of interconnected components. The basic idea is to build software component-by-component rather than instruction-by-instruction.

1.1   Components and Modules

A *software component* is a self contained, encapsulated collection of related concepts, typically providing an abstract data type and associated operations. A component, in turn, forms a partially ordered set of modules that specify and implement the abstractions provided by the component. A *module* is a program unit in a software system that corresponds to a discrete and clearly identifiable region of program text [7]. Figure 1 illustrates these notions. Software modules form hierarchies embodying levels of abstractions and information hiding, two important, complementary, principles associated with component-based development.

Compositional software construction deals with two kinds of structures. The dynamic structure is problem-oriented specifying the system's functionality in terms of interconnected functional modules with a "call-return" semantics in the connections. The *static structure* is the physical organization of the modules in terms of their structural relations specifying, primarily, "import/export" semantics. In this paper we are particularly concerned with the static structure. In the rest of the paper we concentrate on static structure.

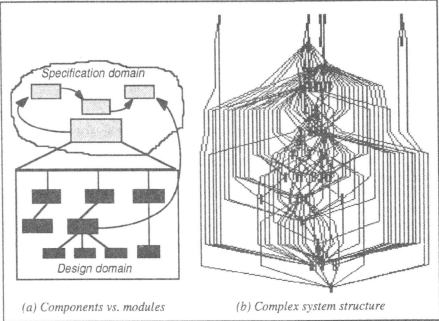

(a) Components vs. modules　　　　*(b) Complex system structure*

Figure 1. *Architectural hierarchies. (a) Interconnected components via "clientship" relations (arrows); interconnected modules via "refinement" relations (straight lines). (b) Modern software systems are too complex to be implemented monolithically and instruction-by-instruction. There are many levels of abstraction, integrated out of a collection of modules component-by-component.*

1.2　Software Static Structure

Today, software understanding goes beyond comprehending individual modules; it requires understanding of the role of each module in the design in terms of its association with other modules (e.g., scope and visibility). The static structure deals with the packaging of software modules in order to facilitate system construction and maintenance, through a clear portrayal of intermodule relations.

　The static structure plays a crucial role in the management of large software systems. This is because there are different ways to "package" the same set of functional modules into a static, build-oriented, structure, since this does not have an effect on the functionality provided. Managing static structural representations involves dealing with abstract layers and refinements, visibility and encapsulation, as well as import/ export and inheritance relations. These aspects may impose constraints on the physical presence of separate portions of the software. (For example to limit imports' scope). The actual coupling between modules in the static structure is not dictated simply by the dynamics of inter-module "calls" and data passing, but by import/export and refinement relations uncovered during the design and development stages. An issue seldom taken into account during design, and in many instances a common misconception.

Many traditional design methods fail to separate dynamic structural components from the more static program text relations. A considerable amount of architectural design effort still remains after the dynamic structure has been determined. It is worth noticing that this additional design effort does not affect the dynamic structure, but the way functional modules can be (re)organized into a convenient set of "manageable components." For example, structured design methods are concerned only with a call-return semantics (subprograms become the main architectural element) incorrectly assuming that this also specifies the best way to organize the program text and to incrementally build the system. Nothing is further from the truth. This situation can be seen even in newly proposed approaches.

Indeed, studying later variations to structured design methods [11, 10, 6], we observed that although they attempt to identify the two kinds of static and dynamic structures, these are treated as one, thus failing to make a distinction between problem-oriented issues and purely engineering or software building considerations. Even in cases where static structure issues are directly addressed [5], this takes place without considerations for incremental development approaches.

We strongly believe that this separation of concerns is important. The fact that systems are developed incrementally increases the need for tight control of this structure in the physical program text. We have discovered that when the implementation language supports the capability to specify static relations in the source text (e.g., Ada), then a given incremental building approach (e.g., top-down vs. bottom-up) must be taken into consideration when packaging the software architecture. Interestingly enough, contrasting structures are generated when following a top-down vs. a bottom-up incremental construction approach for the same design (dynamic) architecture.

The interaction between software development and continued development is strongly influenced by these kinds of issues. Take for instance "maintenance" engineers, they need to recognize and understand design decisions by abstracting program functionality and concentrating on the actual non-linear software text [7].

2   Hierarchical Modular Diagrams

Hierarchical Modular Diagrams, HMD for short, is a module-interface-oriented graphical language capable of showing the static relations among interconnected components. HMD depicts both linear hierarchies of layers of abstractions, and tree-like hierarchies of levels of information hiding. Clientship relationships are shown explicitly, and depicted iconically indicating exactly the place where importing takes place. Refinement relations are also clearly indicated.

2.1   HMD Symbols

The basic graphic principles behind HMD and the diagrams' outline are very simple. HMD uses the same graphical icons and conventions for modules and their elements (called entities) at all levels. The applicability of the HMD to all design elements is part of the inherent simplicity of our approach. In HMD, a module and all its entities are indicated by round (sausage-like) rectangles (Figure 2).

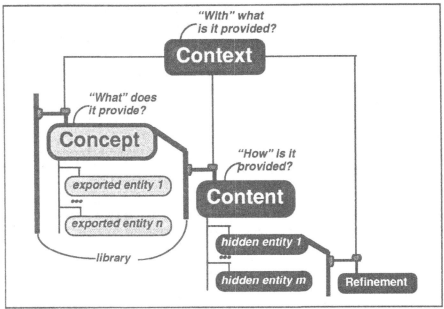

Figure 2. *HMD uses the 3Cs model to completely specify a component [9]. A component, defined by a specification module and a corresponding implementation module, encapsulates exported/hidden entities, which may in turn be further refined, while specifying imported concepts. All connected to a program library.*

Typically, a software component provides an abstract concept with no knowledge of other modules using it. A component is basically introduced by an *interface module* which collectively represents an exported concept specification. Interface modules are connected to a vertical line that functions as a "software bus" or program library into which components are plugged in by a connector (the universal symbol "⌐"). *Exported entities* from an interface module are indicated by connecting them to another vertical line coming from underneath it.

A *Refinement module* is connected to an HMD symbol (parent) by a diagonal line "\" emanating from that symbol. For instance, an *implementation module*, or content, is connected to its corresponding interface symbol. *Hidden entities* of an implementation module are specified in a way similar to that used for exported entities.

Imported components, or context, are shown as dotted HMD symbols connected to the corresponding importing module, indicating the exact place where importing actually occurs (i.e., a specification module, an implementation module, and a refinement module can all import explicitly other components). Parametric information, e.g, for generic templates, can also be shown in this way.

There is no need for complicated displaying algorithms in order to provide aesthetically pleasing diagrams. Designs tend to grow downwards connecting components and entities, and can only expand to the right by providing refinement modules. Import lists of components also grow systematically, upward and toward the right.

Since an important aspect of program text management is to show the structural relations across all modules, HMD limits the number of interactions between modules by restricting the kinds of inter-module relationships. Only three inter-module relationships are directly specifiable in HMD, these are:

• *Provides*: this relation specifies that a component (the provider) makes available an exported component's specification module, whose implementation is hidden. This relation does not yield a hierarchy since the exported module specification is not given separately (by definition of encapsulation), if it were, then this module becomes a provider itself.

• *Refined as*: this relation specifies how a module (parent) is decomposed into a refinement module (child). This relation always defines a tree-like hierarchy from a parent module down to child modules.

• *Clientship*: this relation serves to specify that a module (client) explicitly uses entities exported by another component (the provider). This relation gives a linear hierarchy. Notice that in support for reusability, providers should not know the identity of the modules that import them.

There are a number of very important distinctions between textual notations and HMD, as follows. The iconic nature of HMD puts it in the group of module-interface-oriented languages capable of incorporating concepts from other textual languages. We achieve this by separating design-oriented graphical syntax, i.e., HMD itself, from more detailed module specification syntax as defined by an underlying textual language. In other words, HMD does not really exist in textual form, and thus is not constrained by the syntactical details of a compilable language; on the contrary, HMD is capable of incorporating existing languages. This makes it possible to maintain a bridge between a textual form, say Ada, and a graphical design, which obviously supports both reverse engineering and automatic code generation.

Another point of paramount importance is that HMD makes it possible to specify import lists at the implementation level of a component, including individual local refinement modules, without affecting the specification of the exporting parent module. A major feature of HMD is that any symbol instance can be refined resulting in the introduction of corresponding additional modules; entity refinement allows the association of individual dependencies to particular entities. These capabilities together with a clear indication of separate compilation allows the designer to deal with the notion of extended scopes, so important in large software development efforts, in a two dimensional space.

In many aspects, HMD enhances rather than replaces textual design languages. For example, certain design languages allow the identity of client modules to be known to the corresponding importing modules. Although HMD does not promote this approach, the inner syntax associated with an underlying design language may still allow such coupling to exist. We have done a complete isomorphism between HMD and Ada, Modula-2 and also between HMD and PIC [12], a design language, in order to demonstrate the utility of the technique. See Figure 3.

We used Ada mainly for two reasons. First, we do believe that the language has well-suited constructs supporting many modern design principles for programming-in-the-large. An Ada "program" is a hierarchical collection of compilation units (library units, secondary units, and subunits). Ada allows separate compilation of library unit specifications, library unit bodies (secondary units), and of (local) program unit bodies (subunits). The latter refers to program units (packages, subprograms or tasks) that are declared inside other units with their bodies separately compiled as subunits; this yields a tree-like hierarchy. The importing of library units defines a linear partial ordering which combined with the tree structure of subunits defines the software static structure. These can all be shown using HMD as illustrated in Figure 3.

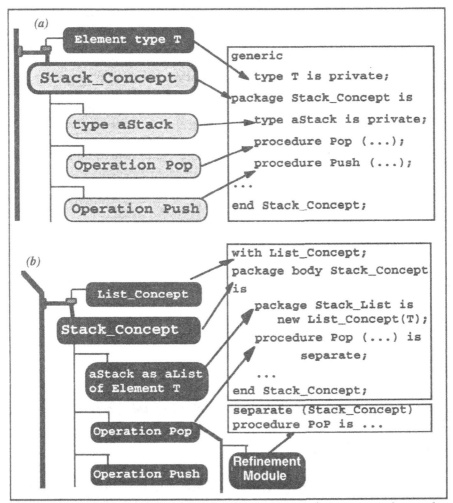

Figure 3. *HMD example of a component specification (a) and its corresponding implementation (b), showing mappings to corresponding textual Ada source.*

The notions of derived types (a limited form of inheritance) and generic units can also be shown using HMD. And second, there is a real need for bringing together these architectural issues and the Ada language to provide a smooth transition from more conventional software development to the correct use of the language. Notice that by refining individual entities we can obtain greater control over visibility of imported concepts. This issue is very important and bares relevance with the newly proposed Ada construct of "child units" (an Ada library unit specified as being part of an existing library unit).

2.2 Static Structure Graphs

The HMD technique is not complete without a dependency graph, called *static structure graph*. This graph presents a summary of the static structure showing the import/export and refinement relations between modules leaving out specifications details and local components (unless these have explicit import lists). The construction and display of such a graph is quite important in software systems with a large collection of compilation units, and has deep implications in several areas. Most importantly it is a first step in reverse engineering an existing project. A static structure graph can show the complexity of the relationships between the various software modules. It can show whether top-down integration, bottom-up integration, or a combination of the two approaches was used during system development. Also, it can drastically effect compilation speed and an optimum compilation scheme can be derived from it. Figure 4 shows a typical static structure graph.

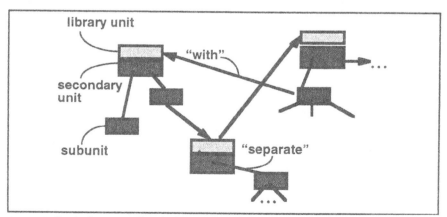

Figure 4. *Static Structure Graph. A summary of clientship and refinement relationships.*

3   Support Tools

Currently, we have implemented a prototype system, called *SSGView*, for reverse engineering Ada software systems (i.e., a collection of Ada compilation units). The system primarily presents a multilevel static structure graph; the nodes on this graph representing compilation units whose contents can in turn be selectively displayed using HMD.

The SSGView tool consists of three parts. A parser for scanning Ada source files (containing compilation units) to build a graph of library units, secondary units, and subunits; layout algorithms for automatic construction of a graphic representation of the static structure, and a Motif/GKS program for displaying the static structure graph. All software was written in Ada, interfaced as necessary to existing libraries. The *Ada lex* lexical analyzer and the *Ada yacc* parser generator [1], driven by a BNF style LALR (1) Ada grammar, were used to construct a parser to scan the Ada files and build graph. *Adjacency lists* [8]were used to represent the static structure (digraph binary files) and Diana Trees to store the parsed Ada code. These two data structures were then used by the graph drawing program.

A hierarchical drawing of an acyclic directed graph is a representation where the vertices and edge bends are required to lie on a set of equally spaced layers and the directed edges are constrained to point upwards. A directed edge means a dependency exists between two vertices.   In this sense, all edges representing the relationship between two modules are directed. If an edge exists, from vertex A to vertex B, then unit B must be compiled before unit A. The edge may be drawn with or without an arrow head, depending on the type of relationship that exists, but it is a directed edge nonetheless. The convention for drawing static structure graphs has directed edges drawn from the unit being imported to the unit doing the importing, and undirected edges connecting subunits to their parents (see Figure 4). Aesthetic criteria [4] for what constitute a "good" drawing are considered as follows: (1) Edges should point in one direction; (2) vertices should be evenly distributed; and (3) there should be as few edge crossings as possible. An example is shown in Figure 5.

An Ada binding to GKS was used. A public domain Ada interface to the OSF/ Motif toolkit was used to provide a more user friendly interface than that offered by GKS. Interfacing a large amount of code between Ada and another high order language presents some interesting problems. The main difficulty in this project was mapping the data structures as defined in the ANSI Ada/GKS [3] specification with the data structures defined in the ANSI "C"Motif specification. Given the existence of the previously developed binding the interface was easily implemented but may be somewhat confusing because it transitions through several layers of libraries and three different languages.

4   Conclusions

The static software structure can be thought of as the packaging of the dynamic structure in terms of software modules. The system functionality is dictated to a large extent by the dynamic structure. The software dynamic structure refers to the thread of execution in the software system; this is characterized by elaboration and activation of the various components and the execution of their actions. In this sense, the dynamic structure is the description of the control flow and data flow between modules and this, of course, has an effect at run-time only. The problem is that earlier structural architec-

149

tural notions were based mainly on the discovery of dynamic elements (e.g., procedures). We strongly believe that architectural design should not be driven by the
dynamics of control flow (this is detailed design), but by static import/export relations.

We have presented a notation to capture static structure information for which we
have developed tools also presented in the paper. SSGView collects certain static structure metrics as a result of our formalization of the static structure elements; these metrics include a system maintainability measure and a component reusability factor.
Although an interactive tool, SSGView does not have the capability of updating the static structure. We are experimenting with a commercially available graphical tool as
HMD's graphical editor to do forward engineering.

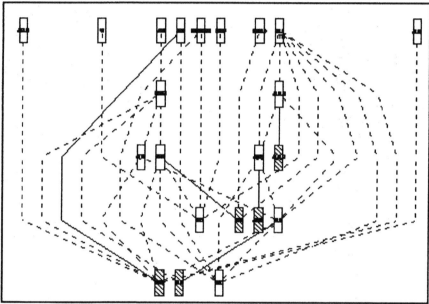

Figure 5. *Parse & SSGView own Static Structure: Non-crosshatched boxes are library
units and crosshatched boxes are secondary units. Solid lines show refinement relationship. Dashed lines show the "clientship" relationship.*

Acknowledgments:

The SSGView tool set was built by Douglas Rupp while he was completing his Mas-
ters degree at George Mason University, he is now at Washington University in Seattle.
The HMD interface was adapted by Edgar Guedez, while completing his Masters at
George Mason, from a system I implemented with Shawna Gregory, now at MITRE
Washington, D.C. Many thanks to all of them.

References

1. Arcadia Project, Dept. of Information and Computer Science, University of California, Irvine.

2. Díaz-Herrera,J.L and R.Flude "Pascal/HSD: A Graphical Programming System" (compsac80: Computer Software & Applications Conference, Chicago, October 1980, pp 723-728)

3. Graphical Kernel System (GKS) Ada Binding, ANSI **X3.124.3**-1989.

4. Eades, P. and L. Xuemin "How to Draw a Directed Graph" Proceedings of the IEEE Workshop on Visual Languages (VL'89), 13-17, 1989

5. Gomaa,H. "ADARTS" (SPC Technical Report, 1991)

6. Nielsen,K. and K.Shumate "Designing Real-time System with Ada" (Communications of ACM vol **30**, no 8, Aug. 1987)

7. Rugaber,S., S.B.Ornburn and R.LeBlanc,Jr. "Recognizing Design Decisions in Programs" (IEEE Software, pp 46-54, Jan. 1990)

8. Tarjan, Robert E. "Depth-first search and linear graph algorithms" SIAM Journal on Computing, vol. **1**, no.2, pp. 146-160, June 1972

9. Tracz,W.J., and Edwards, S. Implementation working group report. Reuse in Practice Workshop, Software Engineering Institute, Pittsburgh, PA. 1989.

10. Wasserman, A.I. et al "The Object-oriented Structured Design Notation for Software Design", IEEE Computer, March 1990, pp 50-63.

11. Watt,D.A., B.A.Wichmann and W.Findlay. "Ada Language and Methodology" (Prentice-Hall, 1979, chapter 16)

12. Wolf,A.L., Clarke,L.A, and J.Wileden "Ada-base support for programming-in-the-large" IEEE Software, March 1985, pp 58-71)

Structured and Formal Methods: An Investigative Framework

Michael G. Hinchey

University of Cambridge Computer Laboratory
New Museums Site, Pembroke Street
Cambridge CB2 3QG, England

Abstract. A framework based on an integration of structured and formal methods is proposed for an investigation of the correctness and appropriateness of structured design methods in current use. Integrating structured and formal methods enables the assignment of a formal semantics to various structured methods and permits a formal examination of their appropriateness. The approach is illustrated by means of a case study – investigating how Jackson System Development can be modified and made more appropriate for use in the design of real-time systems. The approach is valid for any structured design method provided that an appropriate formal specification language is chosen.

1 Introduction

It is now widely accepted that the use of formal methods in the software development process can result in higher-quality systems. Unfortunately, formal methods are not used as much in practice as they might be. On the contrary, much software development is conducted on a completely *ad hoc* basis. At best, it is supported by structured methods such as Object-Oriented Design (OOD), Structured Analysis/Structured Design (SA/SD), Structured Systems Analysis and Design Method (SSADM) and Jackson System Development (JSD).

As these structured methods are ubiquitous, it seems highly unlikely that developers will forsake them for more formal development methods, at least in the short term. This raises concerns over the correctness and completeness of the more popular structured development methods, and an important area for research is in the development of paradigms of software development with increased formality [11], as well as more formal examinations of existing structured methods [2] with a view to validating and improving them.

2 Structured & Formal Methods

If formal methods are to be adopted by system developers, what appears to be required is a means by which structured and formal methods are integrated to some extent.

Some experiments have been conducted in using structured and formal methods in parallel. A certain amount of success has been reported in using this approach in the development of safe and reliable software systems [4, 14]. However, since the more traditional design approach and the formal specification will be engaged upon by different personnel, it is unlikely that the benefits of formal specification will be adequately highlighted. Indeed, as Kemmerer [10] points out, the effects are likely to be negative.

We can achieve a certain degree of integration of structured and formal methods by expressing "classical" (traditional) approaches such as SA/SD and JSD in terms of formal notations.

Such an integrated approach presents two views of a system, which allows developers, and indeed all personnel involved, to concentrate on those aspects that are of most interest to them. Traditionalists and less experienced developers may be happier to concentrate on the graphical representation embodied in various structured methods. Those who understand and appreciate formal specification techniques may alternatively address the equivalent formal specification.

The result is a graphical notation that is easily understood, together with the means to formally prove the correctness of an implementation *with respect to its specification*.

2.1 Formal Investigations

From the viewpoint of this paper, the most interesting benefit of such an integrated framework is that the formal specification may be regarded as giving a formal semantics to the structured design method.

In this way structured methods become more precise and less ambiguous, and it is then possible to reason about those methods. As a result, we may take a formal approach to the review of various structured design methods, with a view to making possible enhancements or corrections if necessary.

We are, therefore, concerned with an integration of structured and formal methods as a framework for the study of existing methods.

We may make use of the notations of formal methods to express the constructs of the design method under consideration, and then use the associated logic system to prove or disprove proposed properties of that method.

This is our concern in the remainder of this paper; the usefulness of the approach is illustrated by means of a case study involving the examination of JSD as a design method for real-time systems.

3 Case Study

Jackson System Development (JSD) [7] is a structured design method widely-used in the development of data processing applications. The method has been recommended for use in the design of real-time systems [15], and certainly it would appear to be quite suitable for this purpose.

Most structured methods are based on a decompositional approach, which requires that a system is fully understood at the outset; this is not normally the case with real-time systems as they are typically large and complex. JSD, however, is based on a constructive approach that synthesizes a description from a core set of processes.

Similarly, most of the real-time design methods that are used in practice (e.g., DARTS, Real-Time Structured Design) and many of the more popular formal methods (e.g., VDM and Z) are based on methods that have basically been developed to deal with terminating non-reactive computation. JSD, however, supports a reactive model of computation, in that it bases the description of a system on the time-ordering of events, and permits the expression of timing constraints.

As a result, a recent book [13] has proposed JSD as a design method suitable for use in real-time and embedded systems.

3.1 Jackson System Development

A JSD specification consists essentially of a distributed network of sequential processes. Each process can contain its own local data, and may communicate with other processes in the network by reading and writing messages on message-queues (buffers), and via read-only access to the local data of other processes [3].

The specification is based around a core set of "model" processes which contain most of the data of the system. Further processes may be added to the specification by connecting them to the model.

Each process is a sequential process which is, in general, considered to be long-running. JSD models are defined in terms of events (actions), their attributes, and a set of processes that describe their time orderings (and by implication, possible parallelism).

Communication between processes in the network is either via data-stream connections or state-vector inspections. The former is used when a model process initiates the communication, the latter when a function process is the initiator so that it may inspect the local data of another process.

Messages are normally assumed to be communicated through specific data-streams allocated to messages of that type, and are processed in a first-in first-out sequence. There is no upper bound on the number of unprocessed messages, and no restrictions on the production of messages. A factor that must always be borne in mind is that there is no guarantee that a message sent by one process will be received by another within a given time period. This can have serious implications for real-time applications.

3.2 Limitations of JSD

The language of Communicating Sequential Processes (CSP) has proven to be too restrictive in expressing some JSD examples; this can be attributed primarily to the fact that CSP is based on synchronous communication, whereas asynchronous communication is the basic primitive in JSD.

Using a variant of CSP that supports asynchronous communication (the Theory of Asynchronous Processes [9]) for a formal investigation, Janet Barnes [1] has encountered undesirable behaviour of a real-time system designed with JSD. It was found that the "Hi-Ride" elevator [7] would refuse to service a floor, or fail to stop at the top floor of a building.

This can be attributed to two limitations of JSD, which must be overcome if it is to be used successfully with real-time systems:

(1) Real-time systems are often safety-critical systems, requiring that the system can react (almost) instantaneously to certain events or circumstances in its environment. For example, in a nuclear-reactor, we would probably want the control system to shut-down immediately when its sensors indicate an abnormally high radiation level (indicating a possible leak).

   However, with JSD there is no guarantee that a message sent on a data-stream will be received by the destination process within a given time interval (recall that infinite buffering on data-streams is assumed). In addition, a destination process might never read from a particular data-stream, as it may be suspended awaiting input on some other data-stream.

(2) In real-time systems, we would normally expect that when a process inspects the state of another process in the system, it inspects the *current* state of that process. For example, a flight-control system might refuse to lower the landing-gear if, on inspecting the process monitoring altitude, it (erroneously) believes the aircraft to be too high.

   In JSD, however, the State-Vector Inspection mechanism returns some state that the inspected process has been in, **not** necessarily the current state. That is to say, out-of-date state-vector inspections are admitted by the JSD method.

For real-time applications such behaviour is completely unacceptable and the be haviour admitted by JSD does not always correspond with our intuitions about real-time sy stems. However, using an integrated framework for a formal investigation, [5] indicates that these problems may be overcome. This enables us to determine (relatively simple) modifications to the JSD model, which results in a structured method that may be used very successfully with certain classes of real-time applications.

3.3 Receptive Process Theory

The language used for the formal investigation of JSD is Receptive Process Theory (RPT). RPT [8] represents a reworking of CSP [6], under the assumption that processes are receptive.

A receptive process models the interaction between a system and its environment by input events and output events. A system can never block input from its environment. Indeed, it must always be ready to receive input (which can arrive at any time) which may lead to undefined subsequent behaviour. Similarly, output ¿from a receptive process can never be blocked by its environment.

Such behaviour makes RPT very suitable for specifying asynchronous circuits and data-flow networks. A very interesting discovery, however, is that the notation of RPT can be extended [5] so that it can be used equally successfully in the specification and design of real-time applications, even though it supports no concept of "time".

Like CSP, Receptive Process Theory is equipped with a sound and complete set of algebraic laws. The process algebra consists of a number of CSP-like operators, and algebraic laws permit the manipulation and proof of properties of process expressions and the elimination of certain operators from such expressions.

4 Expressing JSD in RPT

4.1 Processes

A JSD system consists of a network of communicating processes executing in parallel. As part of the network phase, a System Specification Diagram (SSD) is derived showing the relationships and connections between the various processes in the network.

During its lifetime, a process engages in a sequence of events. As a result it will be in one of a set of possible states at any given instance. To model the concept of a state, a JSD process may be modelled as an RPT process with an output channel s on which it outputs its state every time there is a change in that state. Then the trace of events on channel s represents the history of states that the process has been in during its lifetime.

Any process that is capable of engaging in an infinite number of output events without receiving additional input is considered to be divergent, and is modelled in RPT as $\perp$ (*Chaos*). To overcome such undesirable behaviour, a process must also be equipped with an input channel, say f. Input of messages on f then denotes the participation of the process in the corresponding events, and the trace of events on channel f represents the history of events the process has engaged in during its lifetime.

This gives a process structure as shown in Fig. 1.

A process can then be defined in RPT as follows; let $\mathcal{E}$ denote the set of events that a process may engage in, and $\mathcal{S}$ denote the set of states that a process may be in. Then, the set I of input events is given by:

$$I = \{f.\epsilon \mid \epsilon \in \mathcal{E}\},$$

and the set O of output events is given by:

$$O = \{s.\sigma \mid \sigma \in \mathcal{S}\}.$$

We let x and y range over $\mathcal{E}$ and $\mathcal{S}$, respectively, and can then define process P as follows:

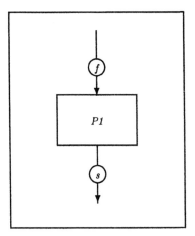

Fig. 1 Structure of a Process

$$P \quad = P_{v_0}, \qquad\qquad \text{for some initial state } v_0$$
$$P_v \quad = (f?x \;\rightarrow\; OUT_{g(x)}), \qquad \text{for } g \in \mathcal{E} \rightarrow \mathcal{S}$$
$$OUT_y = (s!y \;\rightarrow\; P_y \mid f?x \;\rightarrow\; OUT_{g(x)}) \qquad \square$$

4.2 Communication

JSD defines four types of communication primitives, in increasing order of coupling: State-Vector Inspection, Data-Stream Connection, Conversational Constraint, and Controlle d Data Stream.

Conversational Constraints and Controlled Data Streams are normally used when some form of synchronous communication is required. This is not really applicable to the class of systems we are considering here, so we will not address these further.

State-Vector Inspections and Data Stream Connections are of paramount importance, however, as the problems highlighted by [1] are associated with these. For this reason, we now examine how these can both be expressed in RPT. Although Data Stream Connections involve a greater degree of coupling, these will be addressed first, as it is possible to express State-Vector Inspections in terms of these [3].

A **Data-Stream Connection** between processes *P1* and *P2* is denoted as shown in Fig. 2, with an arrow indicating the direction of information flow. The data-stream *s* is a *first-in first-out* buffer with (assumed) infinite capacity. Messages are written to the data-stream by process *P1* and read by process *P2*. Infinite capacity means that *P1* will never block on a write operation. *P2* will block on a read, howeve r, if the data-stream is empty.

In CSP, we might model a data-stream as an infinite buffer, so a similar approach would seem reasonable when modelling the data-stream in RPT.

We assume an input channel *in* and output channel *out* and let

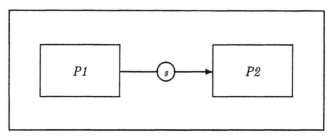

Fig. 2 Data Stream Connection

$$I = \{in.v|v \in \mathcal{V}\} \text{, and } O = \{out.v|v \in \mathcal{V}\},$$

where $\mathcal{V}$ denotes the set of all possible values that will be communicated across the data stream. Let x be a variable ranging over values $\mathcal{V}$, then:

$$
\begin{aligned}
S &= S_{\langle\rangle} \\
S_{\langle\rangle} &= (in?x \rightarrow S_{\langle x\rangle}) \\
S_{\langle v\rangle^\frown t} &= (out!v \rightarrow S_t \mid in?x \rightarrow S_{\langle v\rangle^\frown t^\frown \langle x\rangle}) \qquad \square
\end{aligned}
$$

The process $S_{\langle\rangle}$ is always willing to accept input. It waits until it receives input x and then behaves as $S_{\langle x\rangle}$. The process $S_{\langle v\rangle^\frown t}$ (where t may be empty) eventually outputs value v on its *out* channel and then behaves as S_t, unless its environment supplies it earlier with input x on its *in* channel, in which case it acts as $S_{\langle v\rangle^\frown t^\frown \langle x\rangle}$.

Note, however, that the environment cannot stop S from outputting any or all of its contents at any time. It is more likely that we will want a data-stream only to output its contents when the receiving process is ready to read input.

To attain this goal, we add an extra input channel to the process S, say *test*. We set i$S = I \cup \{test\}$ and keep o$S = O$, as before. In this revised definition, the data-stream can only output data when it receives input on the channel *test* (and being receptive, it is always willing to accept such an input).

$$
\begin{aligned}
S &= S_{\langle\rangle} \\
S_{\langle\rangle} &= (in?x \rightarrow S_{\langle x\rangle} \\
&\qquad \mid test? \rightarrow OUTSTREAM_{\langle\rangle}) \\
S_{\langle v\rangle^\frown t} &= (in?x \rightarrow S_{\langle v\rangle^\frown t^\frown \langle x\rangle} \\
&\qquad \mid test? \rightarrow OUTSTREAM_{\langle v\rangle^\frown t}) \\
OUTSTREAM_{\langle\rangle} &= (in?x \rightarrow OUTSTREAM_{\langle x\rangle} \\
&\qquad \mid test? \rightarrow \perp) \\
OUTSTREAM_{\langle v\rangle^\frown t} &= (out!v \rightarrow S_t \\
&\qquad \mid in?x \rightarrow OUTSTREAM_{\langle v\rangle^\frown t^\frown \langle x\rangle} \\
&\qquad \mid test? \rightarrow \perp) \qquad \square
\end{aligned}
$$

Every process has a vector of variables associated with it; these variables determine the state of the process, and certain events may result in a change in that state. **State-Vector Inspection** involves one (function) process obtaining read-only access to the state-vector of another process in the network.

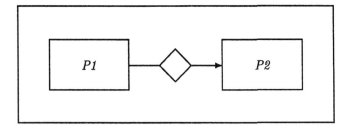

Fig. 3 State-Vector Inspection

Figure 3 shows a portion of a SSD, representing a state-vector connection betwe en processes *P1* and *P2*. Once again the arrow indicates the direction of information flow, so this diagram represents process *P2* inspecting the state-vector of process *P1*.

The reading process cannot be blocked on a State-Vector Inspection, because every inspected process is assumed to stabilize in some state. The value read by the inspectin g process does not necessarily represent the current state of the inspected process, but rather some state that that process has been (or may still be) in. Clearly, this can cause difficulties with real-time systems.

Cameron [3] describes how State-Vector Inspections can be defined in terms of data-stream conections, as shown in Fig. 4.

In expressing state-vector inspections in RPT, we may take a similar approach. Running in parallel with each process *P1*, we define a second process *P1_STATES* which maintains a history of the states of *P1*. Process *P1* and *P1_STATES* are connected via a data-stream *s1*, along which *P1* writes its state to *P1_STATES*. This will in turn output the state it is currently holding to data stream *s2*, in response to requests issued by *P2* along the enquiry channel *e*.

As before, we let S denote the set of states that are to be communicated across channels *s1* and *s2*. We then define the set I of input events as:

$$I = \{s1.\sigma | \sigma \in S\} \cup \{e\},$$

and the set O of output events as:

$$O = \{s2.\sigma | \sigma \in S\}.$$

Then, with $\mathbf{i}P1\_STATES = I$ and $\mathbf{o}P1\_STATES = O$, and letting x range over S, we may define *P1_STATES* as follows:

$$P1\_STATES \qquad = P1\_STATES_{\langle v_0 \rangle}, \qquad\qquad \text{for some initial state } v_0$$

$$P1\_STATES_{\langle v \rangle} \quad = (s1?x \;\rightarrow\; P1\_STATES_{\langle x,v \rangle}$$
$$\qquad\qquad\qquad\qquad | \; e? \;\rightarrow\; OUTSTATES_{\langle v \rangle})$$

$$P1\_STATES_{s^\frown\langle v \rangle} \;= (skip \;\rightarrow\; P1\_STATES_s$$
$$\qquad\qquad\qquad\qquad | \; s1?x \;\rightarrow\; P1\_STATES_{\langle x \rangle^\frown s^\frown\langle v \rangle}$$
$$\qquad\qquad\qquad\qquad\qquad | \; e? \;\rightarrow\; OUTSTATES_{s^\frown\langle v \rangle}), \; s \neq \langle \rangle$$

$$OUTSTATES_{\langle v \rangle^\frown s} = (s2!v \;\rightarrow\; P1\_STATES_s$$
$$\qquad\qquad\qquad\qquad | \; s1?x \;\rightarrow\; OUTSTATES_{\langle x,v \rangle^\frown s}$$
$$\qquad\qquad\qquad\qquad\qquad | \; e? \;\rightarrow\; \bot) \qquad \Box$$

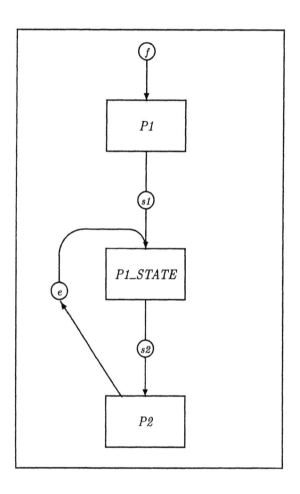

Fig. 4 State-Vector Inspection expressed in Data-Streams

P1_STATES maintains a history of the states that process *P1* has been in during its lifetime. It will continue to discard the oldest state of which it has a record unless it receives input of a new state, or a request (along channel *e*) to output the most recent state. Of course, the definition ensures that where *P1_STATES* records a single state this state cannot be discarded.

Because processes are receptive, we must ensure that where there are multiple input channels, we define the behaviour of each such channel and every message it can carry. As such, we must define the behaviour of *OUTSTATES* if there is a request for the current state before the output has taken place. We decide that, in such an eventuality, the behaviour will be undefined (chaotic) and hence the environment is obliged not to send any further input before the output has taken place.

In the definition of *P1_STATES*, such discarding of old states is possible because in real-time systems we wish state-vector inspection to be up-to-date, and only require *P1_STATES* to return the current state of the process. It makes sense, therefore, to replace the process *P1_STATES* with a process *P1_STATE* which records only the current state.

As before, $\mathbf{i}P1\_STATE = I$ and $\mathbf{o}P1\_STATE = O$, and x ranges over S, so *P1_STATE* may be defined as:

$$
\begin{aligned}
P1\_STATE \;\; &= P1\_STATE_{v_0}, &\text{for some initial value } v_0 \\
P1\_STATE_v \;\; &= (s1?x \;\rightarrow\; P1\_STATE_x \\
&\quad\; \mid e? \;\rightarrow\; OUTSTATE_v) \\
OUTSTATE_v &= (s2!v \;\rightarrow\; P1\_STATE_v \\
&\quad\; \mid s1?x \;\rightarrow\; OUTSTATE_x \\
&\quad\; \mid e? \;\rightarrow\; \bot) \qquad \square
\end{aligned}
$$

It can be proven formally that *P1_STATE* is a refinement of *P1_STATES*:

$$P1\_STATES \;\sqsubseteq\; P1\_STATE,$$

and so we can use the definition *P1_STATE* in place of *P1_STATES*.

4.3   A Simpler Solution

Given that we need to record only the current state, a simpler and more efficient solution is achieved by having each process maintain its own local copy of the state-vectors of other processes it will wish to examine. This is preferable to having a single centralized copy of the state-vector.

Local copies will be updated by having each process whose state must be known output its state whenever there is a change in that state. Since processes are receptive, it is ensured that the local copies will always be fully up-to-date; and the simplified solution is consistent with the definition of a process given earlier.

There is still a problem with Data-Stream Connections, however. Infinite buffering still means that there is no guarantee that messages will be delivered to processes within a given time-period. Again there is a simpler solution.

A process and a buffered data-stream is refined by a process that performs buffering itself, e.g.,

$$(S \parallel P2) \sqsubseteq P2^{BUF}$$

where $P2^{BUF}$ is a process that behaves like process $P2$ except that it buffers input itself. This avoids the need for buffered data-streams, and now data-streams may be modelled simply as channels.

Because processes are receptive, messages will be received from data-streams immediately (apart from propogation delays).

4.4 A modification to JSD

Using the definitions given above, the "Hi-Ride" elevator problem has been completely remodelled in Receptive Process Theory [5].

The solution has proven to be far simpler than Jackson's — State-Vector Inspections have been simplified, and the need for infinitely buffered data-streams has been eliminat ed. In JSD, various types of merge processes are required in an attempt to avoid deadlock; th e RPT solution effectively implements a merge process as part of a standard process definit ion, as a process is willing to accept input on any of its input channels at any time.

The RPT solution is also provably correct, and it can be demonstrated formally that the problems highlighted by [1] are avoided [5].

This leads us to determine a modification to JSD that would make it suitable for use in the design of real-time systems. That is, that JSD processes should be made receptive .

This requires a modification to the way in which processes are described in JSD. To allow for initial input on any of its data-streams, a process's textual description requires multiple entry points, similar to the multiple entry points of an Ada task. We must also allow for the fact that input may arrive on any of the process's input data-streams at any time during its lifetime. This could be handled by adding appropriate Ada-like exception handling.

By making JSD processes receptive, we would ensure that when a message is sent on a data-stream, it is received by the destination process (almost) immediately. Similarly, we would ensure that state-vector inspections are always up-to-date, and enable simpler implementations of these inspections.

As a result, JSD would become equally appropriate for designing both data processing and real-time applications.

5 Conclusions

This paper has proposed a framework for the investigation of the correctness and complete ness of structured design methods, based on an integration of structured and formal metho ds. Employing formal methods allows us to use their notations (formal languages) to determine a formal semantics for structured methods.

A formal semantics makes the design method under consideration more precise; without such a semantics, we cannot reason about structured methods and be assured of their appropriateness.

An example has been illustrated, based on a formal investigation of Jackson System Development using Receptive Process Theory. This has lead us to determine modifications to JSD that would make it more suitable for use in the design of real-time systems, and c orrespond more closely to our intuitions regarding the design of such systems.

Current work involves investigating how specifications expressed in (modified) JSD can be converted mechanically into Receptive Process Theory, as has been done with SA/SD and VDM [12], for example. The result would be a graphical notat ion for real-time systems, that has a formal semantics and which enables proofs of properties and correctness.

JSD and RPT have been chosen merely for illustration purposes. The approach described is suitable for investigating the appropriateness and correctness of any structured metho d, provided that an appropriate formal specification language is chosen.

Acknowledgements

I am grateful to Professor C.A.R. Hoare, who first encouraged me to investigate this area, and to Dr. Mark Josephs for much advice and guidance.

References

1. Barnes, J.: A Study of JSD as a formal design method, M.Sc. dissertation, Oxford University, Programming Research Group, Sept. 1990
2. Bryant, T.: Structured Methodologies & Formal Notations, Developing a Framework for Synthesis and Investigation, In Proc. Z User Meeting 1989, Springer-Verlag LNCS, 1990
3. Cameron, J.R.: An Overview of JSD, IEEE Trans. Software Engineering, Vol. SE-12, No. 2, Februrary 1986
4. Draper, C.: Practical Experiences of Z and SSADM, In Proc. Z User Meeting 1992, Springer-Verlag LNCS, 1993
5. Hinchey, M.G.: JSD, RPT & the Design of Real-Time Systems, M.Sc. dissertation, Oxford University, Programming Research Group, Sept. 1992
6. Hoare, C.A.R.: Communicating Sequential Processes, Prentice-Hall International Series in Computer Science, 1985
7. Jackson, M.A.: System Development, Prentice-Hall International Series in Computer Science, 1983
8. Josephs, M.B.: Receptive Process Theory, Acta Informatica, Vol. 29(1), February 1992

9. Josephs, M.B., Hoare, C.A.R. & He, J.: A Theory of Asynchronous Processes, Technical Report PRG-TR-6-89, Programming Reseach Group, Oxford University, 1989

10. Kemmerer, R.A.: Integrating Formal Methods into the Development Process, IEEE Software 7(5), Sept. 1990

11. Larsen, P.G., Plat, N. & Toetenel, N.: A Formal Semantics of Data Flow Diagrams, submitted for publication

12. Larsen, P.G., van Katwijk, J., Plat, N., Pronk, K. & Toetenel, H.: SVDM: An Integrated Combination of SA and VDM, submitted for publication

13. Learmonth-Burchett Management Systems: Introduction to LBMS Jackson System Development (JSD), Wiley Press, 1992

14. Leveson, N.G.: Software Safety in Embedded Computer Systems, Comm. ACM, 34(2), February 1991

15. Renold, A.: Jackson System Development for Real-Time Systems, Scientia Electra, Vol. 34, No. 2, 1988

An Exploration of Object-Oriented Methodologies for System Analysis and Design

George Yuan, Ph.D.   Nixon Patel

H82/B660, IBM, RTP, NC 27709, USA

Abstract. This paper provides a comparative study of the object-oriented approach by evaluating object-oriented methodologies, and exploring future object-oriented research directions. Six representative object-oriented methodologies are evaluated based on their capabilities in aiding object-oriented analysis and design. The capability criteria used for this evaluation are *object modeling, state modeling, process modeling, object-oriented design*, and *object-oriented model integrity*. In addition to the methodology evaluation, we also discuss some interesting future research, and our work.

1. Introduction

The emergence of highly complicated software systems warrants evolution of new programming approaches. These approaches must help systematic development of quality code for such massively tangled systems which can be easily maintained and reused.

The object-oriented approach, based on object decomposition of systems in analysis and object construction in design, has revolutionized the way the software is being developed by opening various new techniques to fathom the problems arising due to highly complicated systems. This software development approach includes three major phases: *object-oriented analysis, design,* and *programming*.

The first phase is *object-oriented analysis* which is a stage of planning and understanding. In this phase, system analysts and designers work on problem or application domains by decomposing a system into objects, defining classes and their relationships, and providing various models to describe each object's behavior. The major focus in this phase is on "what is to be done" instead of "how to do it." Object-oriented analysis consists of three modeling techniques: *object modeling, state modeling,* and *process modeling*. Among three modeling techniques, the object modeling is the most important one in the object-oriented analysis.

The second phase, *object-oriented design*, transfers models produced in the object-oriented analysis into design models by constructing classes and their specifications, system architectures and configurations, multi-tasking scheme, and implementation principles. In other words, the major focus in this phase is in the solution domains.

The third phase, *object-oriented programming*, is the implementation stage wherein the focus is on programming and debugging for classes obtained in the first two phases. The issues in the object-oriented programming are out of this paper's scope and the interested readers are referred to [Meye88, Stro91].

The advent of various object-oriented analysis and design methodologies is a major step in the direction of object-oriented development. These diversified methodologies, although recognized for their benefits in system development, sometimes make many users confused, due to differences in their modeling capabilities and methods. It is hard for the system developers to select correct methodologies for their applications, and to follow the main stream and right directions of the object-oriented approach.

In order to help users as well as researchers have a better understanding of the latest developments in the object-oriented approach, this paper presents an overview of the current object-oriented development directions, evaluates six representative object-oriented analysis and design methodologies, and discusses future directions in the object-oriented research and development.

The methodologies evaluated are Booch's [Booc91], Coad/Yourdon's [Coad91], Embley *et al.*'s [Embl92], Rumbaugh [Rumb91], Shlaer and Mellor's [Shla88, Shla91], and Wirf-Brock *et al.*'s [Wirf90]. These methodologies reflect the latest development in the object-oriented analysis and design. Methodologies are evaluated based on five criteria, namely, *object modeling, state modeling, process modeling, object-oriented design*, and *object-oriented model integrity*. All the methodologies are discussed based on these criteria in order to have an objective assessment towards their modeling capabilities.

In [Cham92], Champeaux *et al.* give their insights to twelve different object-oriented methodologies by analyzing the differences among these methodologies. In [Mona92], Monarchi *et al.* evaluate twenty different object-oriented methodologies based on the number of modeling issues addressed in each methodology.

Our work differs from [Cham92] and [Mona92] in the following sense. First, we use a different and complete modeling framework for evaluating object-oriented analysis and design methodologies based on their modeling capability. Second, we not only compare methodologies based on the number of modeling issues addressed, but also based on how well these issues are addressed in the methodologies. Third, we analyze each methodology in depth, and explore its modeling capability and integrity, in order to help users have a very good understanding of usability and differences of the methodologies. Fourth, we focus on a small amount of representative methodologies based on the following selection criteria:

- They belong to the object-oriented analysis and design category.
- They are developed for real-time system applications.
- They are well-documented, and users can follow their guidelines easily.
- They must address *procedure*, the steps of accomplishing the modeling, and *representation*, the way of presenting modeling which can be used as communication media for team members and later be used as design documents.

There are many other methodologies meeting the above criteria, but we will not evaluate all of them, in order to have a better focus. The evaluation principles presented in this paper can be applied to others easily.

In the following sections, we will

1. show criteria used for evaluating object-oriented methodologies;
2. summarize the current general trends;
3. review and compare six representative methodologies;
4. explore future object-oriented research directions, and introduce some of our work.

2. Methodology Evaluation Criteria

Methodology's modeling capabilities and integrity are the focal point for evaluation. These capabilities and integrity are crucial to early analysis and design phases. With better modeling capabilities, analysts and designers can describe their systems precisely and completely, instead of paying too much attention to notation and modeling restrictions.

Different methodologies are compared based on the following modeling capability and integrity criteria: object modeling, state modeling, process modeling, object-oriented design, and object-oriented model integrity. These criteria are also the framework which we believe should be used as general guidelines for object-oriented analysis and design.

2.1. Object Modeling

Object modeling, the first and most important step of object-oriented analysis involves understanding problems, setting scenarios, identifying objects (or instances), classes and their relationships, as well as defining object operations. Classes, object definitions or types. and their relationships are sought to understand user system requirements. Usually, a system's data, and static characteristics and structures are captured in this modeling.

In addition to identifying classes and relationships, *domain analysis* is another important task in object modeling. Domain analysis determines which domain a class belongs to in a system. Classes are divided into different layers of domains based on subject matter, public services, low level data management, underlying operating systems, and programming languages. The domain analysis can help simplify the complexity involved in object modeling, have a better object decomposition and system configuration, and enforce principles of separation of concerns.

2.2. State Modeling

Another modeling technique in object-oriented analysis is to identify the control aspect of a system. Every object's dynamic behavior, control, or life cycle are often modeled by a finite state machine (FSM) which consists of events, states, transitions, and actions. This modeling technique is called *state modeling*. The state model can be used to elaborate object behaviors defined in the object model, or to further discover more object operations on its data, and interactions with other objects based on the state analysis. This modeling not only helps define what behaviors an object should have, but also when these behaviors happen to that object.

2.3. Process Modeling

Describing actions in the state model, or operations in object modeling can be done by using a technique called *process modeling*. There are several representations in process modeling. Process specifications, which is the use of high-level pseudo code, is one way to describe these actions and services.

Another way is to use data flow diagram techniques defined in [Ward85]. Data flow diagrams consist of a number of processes, data stores, and data flows. Each process can be further specified by sub-processes, or a process specification.

2.4. Object-Oriented Design

When the object-oriented analysis phase is finished, the next phase is *object-oriented design* which transforms a system's object model, state model and process model into system architectures, class structure charts, class specifications, and implementation principles. Design issues like multi-tasking, use of class libraries, inheritance, class data dependency and access mechanisms, data management, and utilities can be resolved at this phase.

2.5. Object-Oriented Model Integrity

Analysis and design models are built to reflect different views of a system at different design phases, but these views must be consistent, precise, and complete. Otherwise, users may face difficulties in modeling their systems and serious defects may appear in analysis and design products.

3. Object-Oriented Methodologies

3.1. Current Trends

There are two general trends currently in the object-oriented analysis and design. The first one basically focuses on object modeling only. In addition to identifying classes and their relationships, class responsibilities and operations, that is, object *external behaviors*, are also determined at this step. Another major focus of this trend is to discover inheritances and define polymorphism among classes in object modeling. The state modeling and process modeling are treated lightly, or ignored in this trend. This trend tends to have a very concrete definition of objects and classes. This type of methodologies may not fit very well into systems where objects have complicated internal execution controls with frequent inter-object interactions, since these object behaviors may not be well understood and defined at the time of object modeling by just analyzing the responsibilities and services. Booch's, Coad/Yourdon's, Wirfs-Brock *et al.*'s methodologies belong to this methodology category.

The other trend down-plays the definitions of class operations and polymorphism in early object modeling, and focuses almost equally on object modeling, state modeling and process modeling. The state and process modeling is used for characterizing the object behaviors. In this trend, the first step is also to identify objects, classes, and their relationships. Then quickly move into state modeling, and use FSMs to model the dynamic behaviors of each object. Next, the process model is defined to carry out the behaviors defined in the finite state machines. The class operations and interfaces are only defined based on the state and process models. This type of methodology is suitable for complex systems where state modeling and process modeling are also important steps to understand objects' complicated behaviors and control. Shlaer/Mellor's, Rumbaugh *et al.*'s and Embley *et al.*'s methodologies belong to this methodology category.

3.2. Booch

Booch focuses his efforts on the rationale of the object-oriented approach as well as on object modeling issues [Booc86, Booc91]. He gives a plenty of definitions and good examples of objects, object relationships, classes and class relationships, while treating other issues such as state modeling, and object-oriented design lightly. A lot of efforts have been put in using different object-oriented languages to implement his object model.

3.2.1. Object Modeling

Object modeling is one of the strongest points in Booch's methodology, and is the step determining the whole system structure and object behavior. This modeling is involved with several activities: identifying abstractions, understanding the semantic meanings of objects and classes, and creating object relationships and class relationships. Identifying abstractions involves searching for objects in the problem space, and abstract them into classes. Understanding the semantic meanings of the objects and classes is to discover real meanings, like object behaviors, and interfaces, associated with each object. Creating object relationships and class relationships involves connecting all of the objects and classes together, based on the understanding of their behaviors. The class relationships are established according to patterns within object relationships, as well as object *visibility* which determines how objects see each other based on either containing or using relationships. The class inheritance relationships are also defined at this step. Operations and polymorphism are thus defined according to these relationships.

To deal with classes in large systems, Booch suggests using *class categories* to divide classes into groups. A category is a "subject area" representing a set of classes that have some logical relations.

Working products:

- *Class diagram.* A diagram representing classes, and relationships among classes.
- *Class category and visibility diagram.* A diagram showing relationships of classes based on their visibility and categories they belong to.
- *Class diagram specification.* A document including information about class inheritance relationships, its attribute definition, and its operations.
- *Object collaboration diagram.* An object diagram giving a snapshot of object relationships which show object visibility and message synchronization.
- *Object diagram specification.* A document describing an object based on its class name and attributes, and recording messages passed to and from the object based on the operation related to a message, frequency, and synchronization requirements.

3.2.2. State Modeling
Booch mentions in his methodology that FSMs can be used to model an object's behavior, but he treats this issue informally, and leaves it to the readers to decipher the utilization of the finite state machine.

Working products:

- *State transition diagram.* A diagram representing a Mealy's FSM [Meal55] for each class.

3.2.3. Process Modeling
Process modeling is not part of Booch's methodology.

3.2.4. Object-Oriented Design
The issue here is how to implement classes and objects defined in the object modeling. There are two activities involved. The first one is how to represent system execution, and the second one is how to assign classes and objects to program modules and program modules to processors. For the first activity, Booth uses timing diagrams to show object execution sequences and time involved in the execution.

For the second activity, Booch shows that modeling components such as program modules and processor assignment are needed to represent a system configuration, but he does not very adequately elaborate on how to create these components for real projects. Issues like how to convert the state model and how to implement each operation in a class in this phase are not addressed in depth.

Working products:

- *Timing diagram.* A diagram showing the object execution sequences and time involved with each execution.
- *Module diagram.* A diagram depicting the allocation of classes and objects to different program modules in a system. A program module can be a sub-system, a program, or a package of Ada.
- *Process diagram.* A diagram showing the connections of processors, devices and their connections. The diagrams also present the operating system properties which support the user applications. These properties include process scheduling, and other important factors.

3.2.5. Object-Oriented Model Integrity

In Booch's methodology, object modeling is discussed to a certain degree, and is bridged directly to design and implementation. Booch realizes that the state modeling can help in capturing object behaviors, but he does not elaborate on this issue.

It is also not clear how to model operations defined for each class. Booch defines the interfaces and operations for each class, but does not explore this any further so as to address the issue of how the interfaces and operations are carried out. In other words, an important step, process modeling, has been omitted.

3.2.6. Summary

Booch's methodology is helpful in understanding principles of object-oriented development, determining objects and classes, and defining their relationships. It is useful for the construction of small projects where each object's behavior is well known. This methodology is relative weak in system analysis.

3.3. Coad and Yourdon

Coad/Yourdon also pay most of their attention to introduction of basic concepts in object-oriented development. [Coad91]. Their entire methodology is relatively informal, heuristic-oriented, and easy to understand.

3.3.1. Object Modeling

One major focus of Coad/Yourdon's methodology is object modeling. The object modeling is accomplished by identifying objects and classes, developing relationships among the classes, simplifying the model by creating subsystems based on subjects, and defining attributes for each classes.

Coad/Yourdon suggest to use "subject classes" to build high-level abstractions of classes. The guideline is to promote a dominating class to a higher level among a set of related classes, and to make a number of other dominated classes underneath the dominating one. Then these identified dominating classes form a subject class layer. With the hierarchical structure, a system can be analyzed in a simplified view.

Note that the method taken to select dominating classes is heuristic, and the theory itself can be further formalized so as to handle large and complicated systems.

Working products:

- *Class-and-Object diagram.* A diagram depicting classes, abstract classes, and relationships.
- *Class-and-Object specification template.* A document using natural language to specify a class.

3.3.2. State Modeling

Coad/Yourdon suggest that finite state machines be used to depict services of a class. In state modeling, services that a class provides and requests are defined first. Next, message connections are identified between classes. Lastly, a state diagram is built for each service to show the control flow and states in every operation.

This state modeling method (i.e. "service-defined-first, and state-machine-defined-second") is a good approach to modeling object behavior. This method especially fits well into systems where most objects do not have complicated interactions, and object interactions can be easily determined before creating state machines.

The presentation of state modeling in this methodology is informal and light, and the discussion of how to apply the method and notations could be laid down with more clarity so that the users can employ the method and notations effectively and precisely.

Working products:

- *Operation state diagram* (or *service chart*). A diagram showing the control flow and states in the implementation of an operation.
- *Message passing notation.* Graphical arrows from one class to another in class-and-object diagrams.

3.3.3. Process Modeling

Process modeling is not discussed in Coad/Yourdon's methodology.

3.3.4. Object-Oriented Design

The object-oriented design is a phase used to identify additional classes and objects, and implementation of all of the classes [Coad91]. Several factors are taken into consideration in this phase. One is *human interaction*, or human-computer interfaces. The second one is *problem domain consideration* of system timing requirements and limitation of environments. The third one is *task management* involved with multi-tasking, communication, and resource allocations. The fourth one is *data management* dealing with data access and management. Coad/Yourdon in [Coad91] fall short on any attempt to elaborate these important concepts for object-oriented design.

3.3.5. Object-Oriented Model Integrity

Coad/Yourdon's methodology is relatively informal and heuristic-oriented. Some of important models, such as state model and function models, can be further explored. It is also not clear what is the impact of subject layers suggested in object modeling to state modeling and object-oriented design.

3.3.6. Summary

Coad/Yourdon have touched upon a lot of important topics like finite state machines and object-oriented design, but need to explore them in depth. Also application of this methodology to large projects with complicated object behaviors would require extra effort from the users at this time point.

3.4. Embley et al.

A noticeable new comer to object-oriented analysis research is Embley *et al.*'s Object-Oriented Systems Analysis, or OSA in short [Embl92]. OSA stems from Kurtz's Master thesis [Kurt88] and was further developed by students and professors at Brigham Young University [Clyd92].

The distinguishing property of OSA is its emphasis on formalism in some notations, different system views based on levels of abstractions in definitions of classes, relationships, and states.

3.4.1. Object Modeling

Embley *et al.* start the object-oriented analysis by identifying objects, object relationships, classes, and class relationships (a class relationship is called a *relationship set* in OSA). In order to create different levels of class abstractions, the authors suggest using

1. the *relational class*: a class abstracting a class relationship and associated classes as one higher-level class;

2. the *higher-level object-class view*: a higher-level class representing a group of classes;

3. the *high-level relationship-set view*: a class relationship representing a group of relationship sets and associated classes.

Note that there is no concept of attributes in OSA. Embley *et al.* argue that "declaration of attributes at analysis time is premature and potentially harmful to the analysis process" [Embl92].

Working product:

• *Object-class diagram.* A diagram capturing classes, class relationships, high-level class and relationship views, and class participating constraints such cardinality.

3.4.2. State Modeling

In OSA, object behavior is described in a Petri-Net type state machine called *state net*. In a state net, actions are associated with transitions. The state net is *concurrent* in the sense that the machine can be in two or more states or take two or more actions at the same time. Another important feature is that exception handling and real-time constraints can also be modeled in the state net.

To simplify views and modeling to a system, Embley *et al.* recommend *high level state views* by collapsing groups of states and transitions into high level states.

Working product:

• *State-Net Diagram.* A nested Petri-Net type diagram representing the state model for each class.

3.4.3. Process Modeling

Embley *et al.* fail to discuss how to implement actions defined in their state models, and process modeling is missing from OSA.

3.4.4. Object-Oriented Design

Embley *et al.* do not discuss the object-oriented design aspect in OSA.

3.4.5. Object-Oriented Model Integrity

Most existing components in the methodology are consistent and well defined, except that the higher-level class, relationship and state views are defined independently and these views are not well related to each other. The methodology is not yet complete to the development cycle of the object-oriented analysis and design at this point of time.

3.4.6. Summary

One advantage of OSA is its formalism and consistency in most of its basic model definitions, which helps to eliminate ambiguity. The high-level views of object and state models are helpful in decreasing the complexity of analysis and design with different abstractions.

Another advantage of OSA is its different methods for handling higher-level views of abstractions for analysis, but there is more refinement to be done on linkages among these abstractions.

The disadvantage of OSA is that OSA is still a high-level analysis methodology, and some of important components like process modeling and object-oriented design are missing. It is difficult for users to complete their work of system analysis to design without these components.

3.5. Rumbaugh et al.

Rumbaugh et al.'s Object Modeling Technique, called OMT for short, consists of three phases: 1) analysis with object, state and process modeling, 2) system design, and 3) object design [Rumb91]. The latter two phases can be classified into the object-oriented design category.

3.5.1. Object Modeling

Similar to other methodologies, Rumbaugh et al. extensively explore definitions of objects, classes, and relationships. One distinguishing feature emphasized in OMT is that all the relationships, or associations should be treated independently as association classes. These association classes can contain link attributes. The reason for using association classes is to keep systems flexible enough for future changes, and to separate those properties belonging to the relationships from each associated classes. Rumbaugh et al. also associate a number of constraints with relationships such as the class role in a relationship, cardinality, ordering of associated class instances, and propagation of operations through relationships.

Another important feature is that aggregation is modeled as a hierarchical structure, so that an aggregating object representing the whole assembly can contain a number of component objects which are hiding from other objects. Aggregation is a powerful means of modeling the hierarchical real world, and organizing classes in different levels.

When one class depends on another class' definition, Rumbaugh *et al.* emphasize avoiding inheritance relationships by using delegation instead, if the former is not the specialization of the latter.

Note that Rumbaugh *et al.* fail to address how to use domains in object modeling, although the subject is mentioned in their system design, a design phase after the analysis.

Working product:

- *Object diagram.* There are two types of object diagrams. One is the class diagram describing classes and their relationships. The other is the instance diagram showing how object instances are related to each other.

3.5.2. State Modeling

Rumbaugh *et al.* employ a generalized finite state machine notation, Harel's *Statechart* [Hare87], to represent the state model. The notation was developed to model complex event-driven systems, where one state of such a system can contain a number of sub-states which may possibly be independent and concurrent. Here the hierarchical state model helps depict complicated object behavior. The concurrency defined for sub-states allows multi-thread control within one object.

In OMT, events can be expanded into a subordinate state machine. Rumbaugh *et al.* also propose to associate actions, which are supposed to take no time to execute, with transitions and state entry/exit points, and to associate activities, which take durations of time to execute, with states. Although the way of modeling events, actions, and activities is very powerful and rich, in most cases it is unnecessarily too complicated to be fully utilized.

Working products:

- *State diagram.* A diagram describing states, events, actions and activities involved in class state modeling.
- *Event flow diagram.* A diagram showing the external events passed among objects.
- *Event trace scenario.* A scenario presenting some typical examples of event communications among objects.

3.5.3. Process Modeling

In OMT, the process model consists of data flow diagrams which show what happens to object data. The traditional data flow diagrams are used for this purpose. Every process in the process model will be an operation in the class definition.

One problem with the OMT process modeling is that there is no relation between the state model and process model [Rumb91]. Thus, it is not defined in the process model how to carry out actions and activities of the state model. Users are expected to do most of their process modeling from scratch based on the functional decomposition only.

It is noticed that some improvements and changes have been made in Rumbaugh's column in *Journal of Object-Oriented Programming* for the process modeling [Rumb92]. The improvement is to tie the process model with the state model through actions and activities defined in a state transition diagram. For each action or activity in the state model, there is a data flow diagram showing processes defined for the action or activity. The process execution controls and process relationships in the improved process model still need to be better defined. Otherwise, it is not easy to understand the model. Their new approach is similar to those proposed by Shlaer/Mellor before [Shla91], and we will discuss Shlaer/Mellor's methodology later.

Working product:

- *Data flow diagram.* A diagram recording data flows, data stores, and terminators based on the structured analysis technology described in the previous section.

3.5.4. Object-Oriented Design

The object-oriented design in OMT consists of two phases: system design and object design. The *system design* maps out the general system architecture. Concepts of object layers and partitions are used for developing complicated systems. A system can be vertically divided into partitions based on services provided by each of them, and can be horizontally divided into layers based on client-supplier relations. Rumbaugh *et al.* also have discussed how to take advantage of multi-tasking, multi-processor, database, procedure-driven architectures, and event-driven architectures for implementation.

The *object design* in OMT extends models built in the analysis phase into class implementations. Users need to determine what data structures, algorithms and interfaces need to be used for class operation implementation.

In the OMT object design, a number of implementation options are discussed for state model. The options include:

1. implementing a state machine as a control function.
2. implementing a state machine as a separate object which is defined by a state machine class.
3. implementing a state machine with multi-tasking concurrency, if the machine has concurrent states.

Besides the implementation options to the state model, it is also shown how one-way and two-way class relationships are implemented by using pointers or additional relationship classes.

3.5.5. Object-Oriented Model Integrity
Rumbaugh *et al.* have developed three analysis models in depth, but modeling techniques employed are not well related, and can be refined and simplified to be more precise and consistent. The process modeling needs to be further improved to be an effective technique.

3.5.6. Summary
Object modeling and state modeling in OMT are well designed and powerful techniques. Rumbaugh *et al.* also discuss a lot of modeling suggestions, and analysis and design options in [Rumb91]. They also further extend their concepts from design to implementation with implementation options and experiences.

Rumbaugh *et al.* also notice that, for large projects, the current object modeling technique may not be able to handle the complexity. They mention the use of domains such as dividing classes into layers and partitions of class domains in [Rumb91], but they omit any extensive analysis on this important topic. The domain analysis should also be considered in object modeling, in addition to the system design. This domain theory needs to be further refined before it can be used practically.

3.6. Shlaer and Mellor

Shlaer/Mellor's methodology consists of object-orient analysis [Shla88, Shla91a], and recursive design [Shla90, Shla91b] phases. The object-oriented analysis includes object, state and process modeling, and recursive design addresses object-oriented design issues.

3.6.1. Object Modeling
In object modeling, Shlaer/Mellor extensively utilize relational database technology to define classes (called *objects* in their methodology), their attributes, and relationships [Shla88]. The normal form theory is used to determine the boundary of classes, and *entity-relationship diagrams* are used to graphically represent classes and their relationships.

Notice that in this methodology, the aggregation relationship is intentionally omitted, due to the fact that hierarchical structures are not suitable for a relational database schema. There are advantages and disadvantages with this kind of method. The advantage is that every class is treated uniformly as a combination of a table of data and operations on the table. The disadvantage is that a flat model may not reflect some system with intrinsic hierarchical data structures accurately.

In addition to the class and relationship definition, Shlaer/Mellor suggest using domains to simplify object modeling, which will produce a better system configuration [Shla90, Shla91b].

Classes in a system are divided into four layers of domains according to subject matter and service type. Domains can be defined from higher to lower as follows:

1. Application domains. Subject matter in users´ perspective.
2. Service domains. Groups of classes which provide generic services and are application-independent.
3. Architecture domains. Groups of classes dealing with rules and managements of data base, data structures, algorithms, and control handling.
4. Implementation domains. Classes in operating systems and languages.

Classes in lower-layer domains provide services to classes in higher-layer domains. Classes in different domains are analyzed independently with the assumption that services from lower-layer domains are available. Mappings are defined for the services. In the design phase, the requests for the services will be bridged with those services provided according to the mapping scheme.

Working products:
- *Information structure diagram.* An entity-relationship diagram representing the object model.
- *Object and attribute description.* A collection of definitions of classes, their attributes and domains.
- *Relationship description.* A document showing the semantic meaning of each relationship in the object model.
- *Domain chart and mapping definition.* A chart and its description which help to divide objects into different domains based on subject matter and client-server requirements. Mappings are used to describe how objects in different domains can communicate with each other.

3.6.2. State Modeling

In state modeling, state transition diagrams are employed to describe an object's "life cycle," or behavior [Shla91]. An object's behavior is modeled by a Moore finite state machine [Moor56] which consists of a collection of states, their associated actions, and events. Events are the driving forces transforming an object from one state to another. Events to an object can be sent internally by itself or externally by other objects. The inter-object events form the inter-object communications. An *object communication diagram* is utilized to show the communications.

Note that both the Moore finite state machine and the Mealy finite state machine are simple, and easy to use but have limited expressive power in describing complicated object behavior such as concurrent and hierarchical state structures within one object.

Working products:

- *State transition diagram* (or *state transition table*). A diagram describing the state model for each object class.
- *Event list*. A list documenting both the internal and external events of all objects. Information recorded for each event includes its label, meaning, event data, source, and destination.
- *Object communication diagram*. A diagram showing the external events passed between object classes.

3.6.3. Process Modeling

Actions in a state transition diagram are modeled by processes which are connected by the data and control flows in data flow diagrams. There is a data flow diagram corresponding to every action in a state diagram. An action can also be defined by process specifications.

Data flow diagrams can precisely describe actions in state models. Processes in the diagrams turn out to be operations for each class. One minor problem with this method is lack of levels of process abstractions. The model can be quite complicated when actions are complex by their nature.

Working products:

- *Object access diagram*. A diagram showing the data accessing among object classes.
- *Action data flow diagram*. A diagram presenting processes involved with each action in the process model.

- *State process table.* A table recording each process identifier, and its associated object state and action.
- *Process description:* A document specifying each process based on pseudo-code called *process specification.*

3.6.4. Object-Oriented Design

Shlaer/Mellor use a method called *recursive design* to transfer object-oriented analysis products into object-oriented design products [Shla90, Shla91b]. The recursive design accomplish two major steps: bridging object domains, and transferring state and process models into object-oriented design products.

The first step, bridging object domains, is based on the mapping definition defined in object modeling. With the bridges, operations of classes in higher-level domains can be carried out by classes in lower-level domains that are application-independent and highly reusable. Thus, instead of extending the analysis models with new additions of data structures and algorithms, the recursive design just builds bridges across domains, and makes classes in lower-domains highly reusable.

The second step is transferring state and process models into different object design products which will be discussed later in this subsection. Shlaer/Mellor emphasize "cookie cutter" method for object-oriented design in the sense that the class and code can be defined based on several fixed patterns, or software architectures. The only work to be done is to find the right architecture for the project implementation, and to transfer analysis models mechanically into design products. The advantage of formal methods and mechanisms in transferring analysis working products into the design is to reduce human design errors, and to help automated generation of design products.

Design architectures defined in Shlaer/Mellor's methodology is based on principles that a state machine must be included as a front-end for each class. The advantage is that the state model developed in the analysis phase can be used in the design phase. On the other hand, the design method is relatively rigid and leaves users without many implementation alternatives.

Another possible problem with this method is that, in the recursive design phase, classes are the center of activities for a system, and each of them is implemented by a table-like structure, and operations on the structure. An object becomes a row of data in the table with its identifier. This kind of implementation treatment fits into database-type systems well, but extra effort is needed for developing real-time systems with hierarchical data structures, and for implementation in C + + .

Working products:

- *Task communication diagram*. A diagram showing the messages passed among tasks.
- *Class diagram*. A diagram presenting the interfaces for each class.
- *Class dependency diagram*. A diagram describing the data dependency among classes. The dependency can be both message passing and data access.
- *Class structure chart*. A chart representing a class by using modules and data passed between the modules.
- *Class inheritance diagram*. A diagram showing the inheritance relationships among classes within one system.

3.6.5. Object-Oriented Model Integrity
In this methodology, most notations and definitions are precisely and consistently described. It is also easy for users to validate and navigate through the analysis and design products through models such as *object communication models* and *object access models*.

3.6.6. Summary
Shlaer/Mellor's methodology covers most aspects in the development cycle of object-oriented analysis and design. Their working products are consistent and well related. Most notations are defined precisely and formally.

The methodology proposed by Shlaer/Mellor heavily depends on relational database theory. There are gaps between systems with intrinsic data structures and their analysis models, and gaps between their approach and implementation in today's object-oriented system environment. Users should take this into consideration when using the methodology.

Note that some materials in [Shla91b] are not published yet and only available in their lectures. This should be counted as a disadvantage.

3.7. Wirfs-Brock et al.

Wirfs-Brock *et al.*'s methodology places strong emphasis on object modeling [Wirf90], similar to Booch's, and Coad *et al.*'s methodologies.

3.7.1. Object Modeling
Wirfs-Brock *et al.*'s object modeling consists of identifying objects, classes and subsystems, determining object's behavior and its definition called "*class responsibility*," and defining class relationships and object interactions called "*collaborations*."

In this methodology, a system is considered as a group of classes with client and server relations. These classes can be divided into subsystems (i.e. groups of classes which can be viewed as logical units). A subsystem's responsibility is the composite of its classes'.

When identifying a class, its object behavior, or responsibility, is also determined. The responsibility includes what services this class will provide, and what services this class expects from other classes. Each service's definition is specified in a *contract*.

Object interactions, or collaborations, are built based on the services provided by different classes. Aggregations and class relationships are used to illustrate the type of interactions among objects. The interactions are carried out by clients requesting services from servers based on service definitions (i.e. contracts).

This methodology's object modeling is very rich and powerful in defining classes and their object behavior. But note that using the client-server relationship to model all of the relationships is an overly-simplified way to handle all of the possible class relationships and object interactions. The reason is that there may be no client and server in some two-way class relationships where two classes are basically equal to each other. The whole approach taken in object modeling is quite heuristic-oriented.

Working products:
- *Class and subsystem cards.*   Documents recording information related to classes and subsystems.
- *Hierarchy graph.*   A graph showing the inheritance relation among classes.
- *Venn diagram.*   A diagram showing common and individual class responsibilities using Venn notations of the set theory.
- *Collaboration graph.*   A diagram defining object interactions.

3.7.2. State Modeling
State modeling is not a part of Wirfs-Brock *et al.*'s methodology.

3.7.3. Process Modeling
Process modeling is also not a part of Wirfs-Brock *et al.*'s methodology.

3.7.4. Object-Oriented Design
Object-oriented design is a step which refines the object behavior and service definitions specified in object modeling by defining interfaces, called *"protocols,"* and constructing implementation specifications for each class. Work involved in this

step includes class refinements and specifications, class polymorphism definitions, and service specifications.

Object-oriented design is treated lightly in this methodology. More improvements are needed to make this design method really useful.

Working Products:

• *Class and contract specification* A document specifying class definition, and responsibilities.

3.7.5. Object-Oriented Integrity

This methodology focuses on object modeling. Most models described in the methodology is consistent, but they are far from covering all the aspects needed in object-oriented analysis and design. The methodology itself is relatively informal and heuristic-oriented.

3.7.6. Summary

In Wirfs-Brock *et al.*'s methodology, the client-server paradigm is unique and very important, but may not cover all of the possible class relationships. The methodology depends on object modeling only in analysis, thus it may not be easy to apply it to complicated systems, where objects have nontrivial controls and interactions.

3.8. Comparison and Summarization

Table 1 on page xxvi compares the methodologies discussed in previous sub-sections, and summarizes our evaluation. The comparison is based on the criteria of modeling capabilities and model integrity. In the table,

• 0 = Not Defined
• 1 = Poor
• 2 = Fair
• 3 = Good
• 4 = Excellent

Point system depicted below, although approximate, does reflect usability and capability of modeling, based on our evaluation.

It seems that the development of Shlaer/Mellor's, and Rumbaugh *et al.*'s methodologies are relatively more balanced than the others examined for the object-oriented analysis and design at this time point. These two methodologies complement each others in many ways, as shown in our evaluation.

Table 1. Methodology Comparison						
Methodology	Object Modeling	State Modeling	Process Modeling	Object-Oriented Design	Integrity	Average Points (Total)
Booch	3	1	0	3	2	1.8 (9)
Coad *et al.*	2	2	0	1	2	1.4 (7)
Embley *et al.*	3	4	0	0	2	1.8 (9)
Rumbaugh *et al.*	3	3	2	3	3	2.8 (14)
Shlaer *et al.*	3	3	3	3	3	3 (15)
Wirfs-Brock *et al.*	3	0	0	1	2	1.2 (6)

Also note that the average points or total points in the table should be treated with discretion. If a user is merely interested in object modeling, most of the methodologies rated at three or more points for object modeling are good candidates to adopt.

4. Future Research, Our Work and Conclusion

4.1. Future Research

The object-oriented approach is still evolving, and new proposals are coming out every few months. The focal point for future research still remains to be object modeling, since it is the most difficult part in the whole analysis and design process. The key problem in object modeling is creating a correct object decomposition of a system. In order to solve this problem, the following topics are worth further exploring:

- object identification
- domain theory.

4.1.1. Object Identification

Object identification from a requirement is the most difficult job to most system developers. Heuristics are introduced in all the methodologies we evaluated here, but the object identification still heavily depends on experience and understanding of the object-oriented paradigm. It is expected that more research be done in this field to ease the difficulty of object identification.

4.1.2. Domain Definitions

When the number of objects to be handled increases dramatically, it is very important to arrange the objects in such a way that the complexity involved in the object management can be reduced.

Various ways of grouping classes are proposed. Booch suggests class category to organize classes [Booc91]. Coad and Yourdon suggest a subject layer to handle the complexity [Coad91]. Embley *et al.* developed the nested view theory for objects and their relationships [Embl92]. Rumbaugh *et al.* mention dividing classes into layers and partitions [Rumb91]. Shlaer and Mellor recommend a domain theory [Shla90]. Wirfs-Brock *et al.* use subsystems to provide high-level abstractions of classes [Wirf90]. These suggestions all have a similar objective which is to divide classes into different kinds of groups, or domains. Currently, the definitions are quite diversified, and it can be predicted that an increasing amount of focus will be placed on this issue.

4.2. Our Work

We have explored and refined some work proposed by Shlaer/Mellor and Rumbaugh *et al.*. The work is reported in [Yuan93]. Our major enhancements to their work in OOA include

1. modeling through prototypical objects,
2. definitions of class dependency and derived association,
3. state and process modeling of synchronous and asynchronous message passing,
4. state process modeling of inheritance, overloading, generic templates, virtual methods,
5. formalized object, state and process modeling notations,
6. consistency of all modeling techniques,
7. heuristics of transformation of OOA/OOD models into OOP code.

4.3. Conclusion

This paper opens with a conceptual definition of the object-oriented approach. Furthermore, six representative methodologies are evaluated, based on the following five criteria: object modeling, state modeling, process modeling, object-oriented design, and object-oriented model integrity.

Based on our comparison, it is shown that Shlaer/Mellor's, and Rumbaugh *et al.*'s methodologies are better developed than the others examined at this time point because of their well-balanced relatively-complete analysis and design cycles. It is also found that they complement each other in many ways.

The object modeling is considered the focal point of future research in the object-oriented approach. The key problem today with object modeling is still determining the correct object decomposition of a system. In order to solve this problem, the following topics need to be further explored: object model refinement, parent and child paradigm for object modeling, domain definitions, and object organization.

References

[Booc86]   Booch, G.; "Object-Oriented Development"; *IEEE Trans. on Soft. Eng.*; 12(2); Feb. 1986.

[Booc91]   Booch, G.; *Object-Oriented Design with Application*; The Benjamin/Cummings Publishing; Redwood City, CA; 1991.

[Cham92]   Champeaux, D., Faure, P.; "A Comparative Study Of Object-Oriented Analysis Methods" *Journal of Object-Oriented Programming*, Mar., 1992

[Clyd92]   Clyde, S., Embley, D., Woodfield, S.; "Tunable Formalism in Object-Oriented Systems Analysis: Meeting the Needs of Both Theoreticians and Practitioners," *ACM OOPSLA'92*, Oct., 1992.

[Coad91]   Coad, P., Yourdon, E.; *Object-Oriented Analysis* ; Prentice Hall, Englewood Cliffs, New Jersey; 1991.

[Embl92]   Embley, D., Kurtz, B., Woodfield, S.; *Object-Oriented System Analysis: A Model-Driven Approach* Prentice Hall, Englewood Cliffs, New Jersey, 1992.

[Hare87]   Harel, D.; "Statecharts: A Visual Formalism for Complex Systems"; *Sciences of Computer Programming*, 8, North-Holland, 1987, 275-306.

[Kutz88]   Hurtz, B.; *OSA: An Object-Directed Methodology for System Analysis and Specification*; Master Thesis, Dept. of Comp. Sci., Brigham Young University, Provo, Utah; 1988.

[Meal55]   Mealy, G.; "A Method for Synthesizing Sequential Circuits"; *Bell System Tech. J.*, 34, 1955, pp 1045-1079.

[Meye88]   Meyer, B.; *Object-Oriented Software Construction*; Prentice Hall, Englewood Cliffs, NJ; 1988.

[Mona92]   Monarchi, D., Puhr, G.; "A Research Typology for Object-Oriented Analysis and Design"; *CACM*, Sept. 1992, Vol. 35, No.9.

[Moor56]   Moore, E.; *Gedanken-experiments on Sequential Machines in Automata Studies*, Princeton University Press, Princeton, New Jersey, 1956.

[Rumb91]   Rumbaugh, J., Blaha, M., Premerlani, W., Eddy, F., Lorensen, W.; *Object-Oriented Modeling and Design*; Prentice Hall, Englewood Cliffs, NJ; 1991

[Rumb92]   Rumbaugh, J.; "Designing Bugs and Dueling Methodologies"; *Journal of Object-Oriented Programming*, Jan., 1992

[Shla88]   Shlaer, S., Mellor, S.; *Object-Oriendted Systems Analysis*; Prentice Hall; Englewood Cliffs, New Jersey; 1988.

[Shla90]   Shlaer, S., Mellor, S.; "Recursive Design"; *Computer Language*, Vol. 7(3), March, 1990.

[Shla91a]   Shlaer, S., Mellor, S.; *Object Lifecycles*; Prentice Hall; Englewood Cliffs, New Jersey; 1991.

[Shla91b]   Shlaer, S., Mellor, S., *Real-Time Recursive Design*; Class Notes, Project Technology Inc., Berkeley, CA, 1991.

[Stro91]   Stroustrup, B.; *The C++ Programming Language* ; 2nd Ed., Addison-Wesley, Reading, MA 1991

[Ward85]   Ward, P., Mellor, S.; *Structured Development for Real-Time Systems*; Vol.1-3; Prentice Hall; Englewood Cliffs, New Jersey; 1985.

[Wirf90]   Wirfs-Brock R., Wilderson, B., Wiener, L.; *Designing Object-Oriented Software*; Prentice Hall; Englewood Cliffs, New Jersey; 1990.

[Yuan93]   Yuan, G. X.; "An OOAD Approach with a Case Study"; *IBM TR29.1628* (Submitted to OOPSLA'93); Feb., 1993.

Lecture Notes in Computer Science

For information about Vols. 1–1006

please contact your bookseller or Springer-Verlag